PARENTING
FOR
PURITY

**For books or questions
please contact Tom at
singlepurposeministries.org**

TOM HOUCK

PARENTING
FOR
PURITY

WHAT EVERY PARENT MUST TEACH THEIR CHILD TO EQUIP THEM
TO AVOID SEXUAL IMMORALITY, HEARTBREAK AND DIVORCE.

A Division of WINEPRESS PUBLISHING

Pleasant Word (a division of WinePress Publishing, PO Box 428, Enum-claw, WA 98022) functions only as book publisher. As such, the ultimate design, content, editorial accuracy, and views expressed or implied in this work are those of the author.

Unless otherwise noted, all Scriptures are taken from the Holy Bible, New International Version, Copyright © 1973, 1978, 1984 by the International Bible Society. Used by permission of Zondervan Publishing House. The "NIV" and "New International Version" trademarks are registered in the United States Patent and Trademark Office by International Bible Society.

Scripture references marked KJV are taken from the King James Version of the Bible.

Scripture references marked NASB are taken from the New American Standard Bible, © 1960, 1963, 1968, 1971, 1972, 1973, 1975, 1977 by The Lockman Foundation. Used by permission.

ISBN 1-4141-0668-8
Library of Congress Catalog Card Number: 2006901034

TABLE OF CONTENTS

ACKNOWLEDGMENTS

I would like to thank first and foremost my Lord and Savior Jesus Christ who mercifully rescued me from the world's destructive system of relating to the opposite sex.

Next, I extend my most sincere gratitude to my wonderful wife, Lisa, who spent countless hours over the years helping me in so many ways. She was always there to encourage me through my writing endeavors and was a tremendous support by her like-minded beliefs.

Special thanks goes out to Julie Keating, at that time a member of our singles ministry, whom God spoke through when she told me, "You should write a book." That was something I never had considered. I often joke, "I was voted by my high school class as the one most likely not to write a book on love, sex, or marriage." It was Julie's encouragement that first caused me to see where God was leading me.

Finally, I must thank the people who helped organize and develop my thoughts into written material. Listing them in chronological order, I would like to thank:

Kay Britten of Kay Britten Communications, my public speaking instructor. Kay was the first person to help me tackle the mounds of notes I had accumulated over the many years of single's ministry;

Meg Rensberry who really helped me develop organization in my outlines. Much thanks to her.

Barbara Robidoux of The Christian Communicator Manuscript Critique Service staff, who skillfully and miraculously transformed my written material into what I was really thinking. I can't thank Barbara enough. She was truly a Godsend in making this book possible.

Also, I must thank the many people who fed me valuable input after reading the many versions of this book along the way.

May God bless all our efforts in His name!

FOREWORD

As a singles pastor of fourteen years I spent a lot of time immersed in the world of single adults. When I first began pastoring I was newly married, so what it was like to be single was fresh in my mind. I understood the process God had brought me through when He transformed my life from worldly singleness to godly singleness. It didn't take me long to see that what I would be spending most of my time doing as pastor was helping the people I was ministering to deal with their unwanted baggage of the past and misconceptions about singleness. I was convinced this would be my lifelong calling and never imagined ministering to any other group of people.

The first time I was asked to reach outside of the single adult arena was to speak to a group of high school students at a local Christian school. I felt as though I was in familiar territory as the message remained the same. I didn't see much of a difference between speaking to the teens or speaking to single adults. But then I was asked to share my message with elementary school children.

As I prepared for this meeting I was forced to think of romantic relationships from a child's perspective, not my familiar, single adult's view. The major difference I noticed was there was no need to address how to deal with past baggage in this group. My realization was, "If children were taught this message early, they wouldn't have to have their minds renewed later in life."

The concept was good, but after a couple of meetings with this age group I discovered that it would be very difficult to share this information with children if their parents were not on the same page. This insight inspired me to reach out to parents in order to teach children God's plan for singleness. This book is the product.

CHAPTER 1

WAY OFF TRACK

The Divorce Epidemic

Parents today must be acutely aware of one of the dangers children will face in life, and know how to protect their children from that danger. Our country is in the midst of a divorce epidemic. I say epidemic because we have had a fifty-percent divorce rate for more than thirty years—an extremely high percentage for far too long. Statistics tell us that each year, since 1974, over one million marriages in the United States have been dissolved.[1] Combine that with the additional one million children[2] who have had their lives shattered in the wake of two million adults who were divorced in each of those years. Multiply that times the number of years it has occurred and you have tremendous human tragedy.

We must ask ourselves how did we get so far off-track? We, as Christians, would like to blame secular society for this epidemic and not want to accept any of the blame ourselves. The truth is

[1] CDC
[2] Micheal McManus

that we are more than slightly responsible for causing this. Many Christians believe the secular society has a much higher rate of divorce than the Christian community does, so of course their conclusion is that non-Christians are to blame for the epidemic. Such thinking incorrectly excuses Christians from their responsibility. In reality—although hard for us to believe—the George Barna Research Group reports that there is a slightly higher percentage rate of divorce among Christians than non-Christians. According to Barna's statistics, out of the fifty-percent of marriages that end in divorce, Christians are involved in slightly over half of them.

Why these serious and astonishing percentages? The most common reason there is so much failure in marriage is because of the unbiblical relationships people engage in prior to marriage. Those unbiblical relationships are the result of crossing boundaries God created for us to use when relating to the opposite sex. We have crossed those boundaries slowly over time as we have broadened our liberties in how we relate to the opposite sex. In order to stay within God's protective boundaries we must use His more comprehensive view of what is sexually moral behavior between the sexes. To protect our children from the divorce epidemic we must instill in them a biblical view of sexually purity.

Christians have copied the non-Christians in male/female relationship matters and haven't practiced biblical standards. For the most part, we haven't adhered to God's standards because we haven't been discipled in them. The worldly standard has replaced the biblical standard in our dating practices. In essence, dating, as it is typically practiced, is divorce practice. Therefore, the Church is experiencing the same failure rate as the rest of society. As the saying goes "garbage in, garbage out."

The Church has relinquished its role as the salt and light in the marriage and family area. It has conformed to the world's image rather than being transformed into the image God originally intended. So, rather than the Christians having an effect on the world, the world has had its effect on the Church. If we had been leading instead of following, this epidemic would not have happened.

It grieves me that many Christians are apathetic toward the divorce epidemic. Many of us have become desensitized and have thus accepted the current condition as being a normal and acceptable way of life. It doesn't have to and shouldn't be this way! A fifty-percent divorce rate should be an extremely alarming statistic. It should be unthinkable. Rather than a nonchalant acceptance of it as normal, it should bring us to tears of repentance.

"I'm not apathetic," you tell me. "I care."

You verbalize that and believe it to be true. But apathy expresses itself in inaction. Each one of us can be considered apathetic if we are not doing something to prevent divorce in our own life and in the lives of others.

I have witnessed firsthand the apathy of a community toward solving the divorce epidemic. Years ago, I heard a radio advertisement for a seminar for Detroit metro area pastors and Church leaders. The topic: "How to Reduce the Divorce Rate in Your Church and Community." I responded quickly to the invitation. Due to the tremendous need for such a seminar, I expected a large turnout and looked forward to working with other leaders. I hoped we could begin to make a greater difference in our community. But instead of being part of a large crowd, I was one of eight who attended. Why? Apathy.

Other people ignore the issue because of self-centeredness "As long as it doesn't happen to me, I don't care about it." Or, out of pride think, "the reason it is happening to other people is that they are not as good as I am." Some excuse themselves from personal concern by believing, "If it does happen to me, it's no big deal, I can be forgiven." Such a self-centered belief does not concern itself with the other person's well being. The truth is divorce never affects just one person.

Once I asked a fourteen-year-old if he was going to do anything in his life to prevent divorce. I expected a positive response in light of the pain he had suffered when his mother divorced his dad and married someone else. He answered me with a positive, "Yes!" So I asked the next question: "What are you going to do?"

"I don't know," he answered.

"If you don't know what to do, then you won't do anything to prevent it," I told him.

He wanted to make a difference, but before he could he had to make an effort to find out how. Wanting to prevent divorce is not enough, each of us must know what action to take.

As Christians, we often feel divorce is not in our future so we don't need to concern ourselves with the problem. I have asked many singles of all ages and in various Christian groups, "How many of you think that someday you'll be married?" Typically, everyone raises his or her hand. Then I ask, "How many think one day you'll get divorced?" Usually—and only as a joke—one person will raise a hand. Then I tell them that, statistically speaking, half of them are wrong!

We have been lulled into a false sense of security. We think that just by being a Christian we are automatically protected. After all, divorce happens to other people; not to good, practicing Christian couples, and children who are brought up in the faith will follow the right path and create happy and life-long marriages. That's true, isn't it? Not always! Parents should know that divorce can happen to anyone—Christian or non-Christian. It happens to those who don't take specific steps to prevent it.

Even if divorce would never be a part of someone's life, as Christians we should be concerned over the effect that it has on other people's lives. We are to be our brothers' keeper and never are we to harden our hearts toward them. So even if you don't think this problem concerns you, you still should respond to the heart of God and show compassion for those who are presently hurting or could get hurt in the future.

Responsibility to Solve the Epidemic

Considering the seriousness of this epidemic, it amazes me to see how little effort the Church has put forth to try to solve this problem. Of course, there has been some effort, but, not nearly enough. If fifty percent of the married couples in this country had cholera, would we just accept that and not seek a solution to the dramatic increase? Of course not! We would at least check the drinking water. The divorce epidemic will continue until something is done about it; it will not stop by itself. Are we expecting secular society to stop it? That would be highly unlikely! *Stopping the divorce epidemic is the responsibility of the Church.*

Unfortunately, fear has caused many of us to shy away from attacking the divorce epidemic head on. Some don't want to get involved in such a sensitive issue. After all, isn't this how John the Baptist lost his head? The worldly view is that this is a private affair and we should keep out! With so many divorced people in our midst, we are apt to offend someone without meaning to or even knowing that we have.

The Church must shoulder the responsibility for what it has done to create the epidemic. It must bear the responsibility in a way that doesn't just stop with being guilty alone, but by taking immediate action to correct the problem—doing what it should have been doing all along. 1 Peter 4:17 tells us: *"For it is time for judgment to <u>begin</u> with the family of God; and if it begins with us, what will the outcome be for those who do not obey the gospel of God?"* Change has to start with the Church. 2 Chronicles 7:14 adds: *"If <u>my</u> people, which are called by my name, shall humble themselves, and pray, and seek my face, and turn from their wicked ways; then* *will I hear from heaven, and will forgive their sin, and will heal their land"* (KJV). Healing comes from us doing our part.

We need to adopt the same attitude toward divorce as God has. God hates divorce! God hates divorce in a *constructive*, not a destructive way. He hates it for what it does to His people (see Malachi 2:16). Please understand me: God does not hate His children who are divorced; He hates the destructive process of divorce. I also am not against people who are already divorced; such an attitude or bias doesn't solve a thing.

In light of God's viewpoint on this subject, how can we Christians possibly remain apathetic about this problem in today's society? (See Amos 3:3.) Each of us must become part of the solution. We should help to solve the problem. The constructive way to do this is to concentrate on divorce prevention. We must teach people to honor marriage and protect the family unit.

Knowing What Action to Take

To know what action to take in solving the epidemic we must first thoroughly investigate what marriage is biblically all about. We must see where we are failing and not rush to conclusions based on what is currently believed about marriage. To understand marriage we must recognize it as a building process not an event. A successful marriage is based on the completion of all phases of the building. We must consider what needs to take place prior to a wedding, that is, during the preparation stage, while each person is still single.

Prevention is the key to the cure. We need to prevent divorce from happening in the first place. Helping people who have troubled marriages is important, but that alone won't have as great an impact as preventing inferior marriages from taking place. The greatest opportunity we have to prevent divorce can be found during singleness. It is at that time that the connection between the misuse of singleness and divorce must be realized. To accomplish this, the truth about biblical singleness must be taught.

Typically we think of families as beginning once a couple is married. In doing so we ignore the ingredients that make up the family. All marriages start with two single people. It is their beliefs and values that shape the foundation of the future family. In other words, the foundation of the family is shaped during each of the two partners' time of singleness.

It makes sense to look at singleness from a marriage perspective, to determine what is required during singleness to produce a great marriage. When these requirements are met while the future partners are still single, then the wedding day becomes an acknowledgment of what has already taken place in their lives, providing a great foundation for their future.

A wedding, by itself, has no life-changing ability. It does however provide plenty of opportunities for change. It is harmful to delay any necessary changes to have a great marriage until after the wedding day. All qualities that would provide for a great marriage should be practiced during the single years.

In an interview, a woman said she had been married for eight years and then got a divorce. I thought, *If you and your husband had really been married in the true sense of marriage consistently during those years you would not be divorced now.* Divorce is not sudden and without cause, it is a process just like marriage is. The truth is that during part, if not all, of those eight years the process of divorce had to have been taking place. The seeds were being sown. The real question is, when were those seeds sown? Were they sown during those years of marriage, or were they sown during the single years? My answer: Most likely when they were single.

Wrong ideas and opinions learned over the single years construct the wrong foundation for marriage. Even though the cracks in the foundation are undetected or ignored before the vows are taken, they eventually split open and cause big problems. The early stages of the divorce process consist of an accumulation of lies and the corresponding reactions to them. Believing even one lie, even one wrong belief about marriage can lead to divorce.

When we look at marriage from this perspective we can see the link between biblical singleness and a godly marriage versus worldly singleness and divorce. How vital the time of singleness is to a person's maturity! Biblical singleness creates opposite sex relationships that instill faithfulness, sexual purity, responsibility, and trust—all vital to the marriage bonds.

I used to think that the Bible didn't have much to say about the subject, but I was so wrong. When I was a Christian single—over twenty or so years ago—I began to study what the Bible has to say about singleness to help myself get through those years. I'm still studying with no end in sight; that's how much there is!

When I discovered what the Bible had to say about the subject, I realized that unbiblical singleness and marriage are incompatible. I began to see that the root cause of divorce is the misuse of singleness. I concluded that biblical singleness contributes to the success of marriage. Then, when I compared biblical singleness to how I saw most Christians living their single lives, I found a vast difference between the two.

Often, when people search God's Word to discover what He says about opposite-sex relationships, they don't find the right instructions because they are looking for answers to questions that are not based on God's plan for relationships. Subsequently, there is a lack of accurate teaching from the pulpit about this subject. Our society has filled this void with unbiblical standards taught through print media, television, movies, friends and well-meaning relatives who don't know the biblical standard. Proverbs 18:17—*"The first to present his case seems right,"*—warns us of what happens when someone allows the acceptance of what <u>seems</u> to be true without knowledge of the biblical viewpoint. We Christians need to learn how to discern the truth about relationships. We must not base our understanding upon experience, popularity, or acceptance. We must follow the biblical viewpoint of relationships to combat the worldly view we have become accustomed to.

Divorce is Preventable

Divorce is a needless tragedy. We can't stand idly by expecting that someday the epidemic will go away all by itself; it won't. It will continue until we do something about it! Thankfully, we hold the power to change our world; unfortunately we are not using that power. *"He who heeds discipline shows the way to life, but whoever ignores correction leads others astray"* (Proverbs 10:17). We Christians must follow God's instructions, discipline ourselves, change in the areas we need to change in, and bring that much needed change to our society by example. We can and must make a difference!

Chapter 2

Parenting for Purity

Parental Influence

Parents, you can use your influence to save your children from broken hearts and emotional scarring that come from worldly relationships. Many years ago in our Single Adult Ministry, a mother and father came to me concerned that their daughter didn't have a boyfriend. They asked if I could "fix her up with someone."

"I'm not the matchmaker, God is," I told them. Tragically, that girl came to me a few months later and announced she was pregnant. I wonder how important her parents felt it was for her to have a boyfriend then.

Parents are the most influential people in their children's lives. Who better, then, to teach them about biblical opposite-sex relationships? But some parents have given away their influence. This teaching is designed to help you get it back.

Like it or not, negative beliefs and values concerning male/female relationship issues are being taught to children at early ages. Our children are being programmed to travel down a road of unbiblical beliefs toward a lifetime of sexual immorality and, in many cases, divorce. Parents, other family members, media and classmates are sending false messages on the subject, often without recognizing they are.

Therefore, parents must begin to counteract these teachings by discipling the truth about opposite sex relationships also at an early age. We need to shape our child's values early, because the world is. And why give the world's system a head start? In today's world, children—even as young as those in kindergarten—are under pressure to have a boyfriend or girlfriend. Therefore it has become crucial for even parents of preschoolers to educate themselves on the biblical approach to this topic.

Not only does early involvement help to combat the world's system, it also strengthens the parent/child relationship. Often when a teenager rejects a parent's involvement in this area it is not because of the instructions being given; it is because the conversation feels unnatural since the topic has never been discussed before. If the parent had been involved in this area throughout the child's life this conversation with their teen would not be viewed as an intrusion.

Covering All the Bases

Parents sometimes do not fulfill their responsibility to disciple their children in biblical opposite sex relationships correctly, either they do it incorrectly, or not at all. They often minimize the topic, neglect it, or avoid it altogether. I've heard parents say, "My child is not going to date until she is thirty." Of course, this is neither a realistic nor a legitimate action plan. It is merely another way of avoiding the issue. Parents should view opposite sex relationships as a God-ordained part of life and should see it as a positive topic for instruction and discussion rather than a negative issue to be avoided.

Some parents are deceived into "thinking" they have adequately covered this subject. Believing that it is sufficient to tell children not to have sex before marriage is simply not enough. Children need to know why certain actions and beliefs are immoral to understand what is morally right. They need to understand the principle behind the rule. This explanation should not be viewed as giving in to a defiant questioning of authority, but rather as a child's need to understand what is moral that will enable them to avoid sexual immorality. It is impossible to give your child enough rules to replace the effect of a grounding in principles of sexual morality.

It amazes me that so many Christian parents seem to think their children are prepared for life's battles when they haven't equipped them with God's Word on a particular subject. We wouldn't think of facing the secular onslaught without God's Word on every aspect, yet many of us send our children out to do battle without the proper armor or ammunition. 2 Peter 1:3 tells us we have been given everything we need for life and godliness through our intimate knowledge of who Jesus Christ is. Therefore, since this subject of opposite sex relationships is definitely a big part of life, God must have included instructions for us in His Word.

Sometimes parents procrastinate with these instructions, "Dad can I have the car keys, I'm going on a date," shouldn't be the signal to begin training. One conversation I dread to have occurs when parents come to me looking for relationship advice for their older teenage child. Any sentence that begins with "I have a seventeen year-old daughter and there is this boy," rarely means good news is to follow. The reason I regret having that conversation isn't because I don't want to help—I still do—it's because I know that this is one problem that could have been avoided if biblical parenting would have taken place much earlier in that child's life.

Unfortunately, for some parents this is not an option. They find themselves in a position of not discovering the biblical truth about opposite sex relationships until after their children are already teenagers. While this makes the training more difficult, those parents still must tackle the subject as an essential part of their parental responsibility.

There are others who falsely believe that by discipling their children in other areas of conduct they have covered this one. That's like teaching English and geography while believing that a person will also learn math in the process; they are each uniquely different subjects. Such wishful thinking comes from what is assumed to be an embarrassing subject. It can be embarrassing because of the instructions that have been traditionally taught. We have been more concerned with the biological functions of sex than with God's plan for the relationship. If biblical instructions about the purpose of sex in relationships are used, these relationship conversations need not be embarrassing. In addition to explaining God's purpose of sex in relationships the age appropriate discussions concerning biological functions must be shared, but now they will be less intrusive because they will now be viewed in the context of love and marriage.

Parents may faithfully take their children to Church, pray with them, and teach them in many areas of the Bible. However, if they have not also covered the topic of opposite-sex relationships, they have failed in a vital area of instruction and discipline. A child can be lost in an instant, either temporarily or permanently, to an opposite-sex relationship that is not of God.

A mother of a sixteen-year-old girl was overheard telling someone she "hoped" her daughter wouldn't get involved in sexual experimentation. "After all," she bragged, "Paul and I have raised her right." My response to that statement was, "Did you actually train her in the concept of sexual morality?"

Divorce Prevention

Children today have been unfairly burdened with the dilemma of a divorce-crazed society. It is a serious epidemic in our country and we should be taking measures to protect our children from it. Parents must concern themselves with the fact that divorce **could** affect their children and learn how to protect their children from divorce, not just hope that it doesn't happen to them. We must teach them that it is only through believing in God's precious promises that we escape the corruption in the world (see 2 Peter 1:4).

Unlike forty or more years ago, divorce has now become an integral part of society's fabric. The mass acceptance of this destructive practice is rooted in our common dating practices that are based on false ideas of how to relate to the opposite sex. With divorce and other unbiblical opposite sex relationships being so common for such a long period of time, those beliefs and values have become less noticeable. Wrong now seems right. It is highly likely that those secular beliefs and values may be a part of the parent's life. If they are, chances are they will be transferred to the child. This trend in society is a vicious cycle that today's parents are responsible for breaking. *The best cure for sexual immorality and divorce is biblically informed parental involvement.*

Discipleship Parenting

The parent's responsibility is to provide correct biblical beliefs and a strong value system early in a child's life. It is not job of the youth pastor, or the public school's sex-ed program. We must return to the days when parents exercised their authority. They were the gatekeepers who protected children from the influences of an ungodly world view. They determined what music their children listened to, what movies they watched, and even more importantly, what friends they associated with.

Many of today's parents seem to have lost their compass. They need to step up and take responsibility for the moral health of their children, not excuse themselves from it by blaming others for their failures. We must stop blaming the altered social mores and fight for our own. We must disciple our children, not merely complain about their actions. Have you heard parents complain about their child being spoiled? I always want to ask, "Whose fault is that?" Children can't spoil themselves. Taking responsibility for a child's spiritual development is biblical parenting, doing whatever it takes to see their child succeed. Biblical parenting is not merely the ability to coexist in the same house with the least amount of inconvenience or friction. Some parents don't have a ministry home with biblical roles being followed; it's a hotel where people stay without responsibilities toward one another. True parenting is biblical discipleship. Godly parenting includes discipling children in biblical opposite sex relationships. Parents have been given a tremendous responsibility to disciple in biblical opposite sex relationships; sadly most don't even know how. There are only two choices, either you are preparing your child to have biblical opposite sex relationships or you're not. There isn't a third choice.

It used to be that parents were involved in the child's mate selection process. The father, being the protector of his family, would interview any man who showed interest in his daughters. Dad would put the suitor on the spot by asking him if his intentions were "honorable." He wanted to know if this young man saw the relationship as leading to marriage. He was the protector of his daughter's moral status, her reputation in the community, and her future. Sadly, most fathers have relinquished this responsibility and by so doing have exposed their daughters (and sons, too) to heartbreak and ruined lives.

Children need to be trained in God's method of choosing a mate. They need to be shown the biblical truth that God has created a specific person for them to marry. They need to receive the biblical teaching that it is God's responsibility to bring them together with their mate. (More detail on this in chapters four and six) They must be trained to guard themselves from creating their own desires for just any person which will dull their hearing and make it more difficult to recognize God's revelation of who that specific person is.

Parents are not supposed to hear God's voice for their child as to whom their mate is. I am not talking about arranged marriages. The parent's job is to help to guide their child in knowing if they have truly heard God. This shouldn't be the first time there is any guidance in hearing God's voice; it should be a common occurrence that has taken place throughout their lifetime. Please, don't assume that your child should get married and thus pressure him/her into doing so. Be careful not to allow your desire to become a grandparent to override your desire for God's will in your child's life.

Training Pointers

So how should parents disciple their children to help them avoid sexual immorality and prevent divorce in their adult future? In the early, pre-school years, little instruction is given to the child. It is the parents that should biblically educate themselves on the subject. It is impossible to disciple someone on a topic you don't understand. Be open to the truth, and take time to research what the Bible has to say about it. Then provide the correct example, instructions, and encouragement. It is your conviction not your opinion about this subject that will provide the greatest impact on your child.

It is essential that parents keep from projecting non-biblical beliefs through their actions or words. Avoiding actions such as pointing out a cute child to your child and suggesting the two of them would make a good couple. Stay away from and discourage such comments as "Don't they look cute together", or "Do you have a boyfriend/girlfriend yet?" When parents make such seemingly innocuous comments, the child is being trained to see opposite sex relationships as a game to be played. Pay attention and you will find that this subject comes up more often than you would think. Use those occasions as teaching opportunities to privately and gently instruct your child in a way not to bring them embarrassment or shame.

One father coached his daughter how to respond to such comments. When her grandfather teasingly asked this five-year-old if she had a boyfriend yet, her answer was, "That's not God's way, Grandpa!"

At this stage, little has to be discussed. Just simple comments like "God wants boys and girls to be just friends", or "A boyfriend/girlfriend is a special relationship that God wants you to save for the one you marry." When a boy in first grade tried to kiss that father's little girl, he told her that the only boy she should kiss before she gets married is her Daddy.

In the six-to-ten-year-old age group, tell your child God has a plan for their life. Mention repeatedly and sporadically throughout the years that He has a special person already picked out for each one of them to marry. Instruct them to save themselves for that person. Explain to them in a way they can understand what it means to be emotionally abstinent. Such reinforcements of the biblical ideal must be voiced repeatedly as a constant reminder; we can't check this off the list as being completed after telling them once. As with many instructions in life we need to be reminded throughout life to reinforce them.

People at any age do not need encouragement to develop an interest in the opposite sex. It is not necessary to sustain a heightened interest over the years prior to marriage, as we have been pressured to think. Some parents will promote harmful opposite sex desires to assure themselves their child does not have a desire for the same sex. Three times in the Song of Solomon it advises us that "love must not be awakened before the right time" (Song of Solomon 2:7; 3:5; 8:4). Until then we must teach our children to "guard their hearts" as required in Proverbs 4:23. At the appropriate time God will provide the necessary incentive to spark interest in one particular person.

Children, especially teens, who get involved in emotional entanglements are at risk. It is accurate terminology when romantic liaisons in the early teen years are referred to as a "crush." That's exactly what it ends up doing, crushing the child's innocent heart. God never designed or intended us to have more than one romantic relationship, let alone a series of intimate relationships either emotionally or physically. So it's no coincidence that people get broken hearts when they give their hearts indiscriminately and for the wrong purpose.

Parents must encourage their children to remain emotionally faithful to their future spouse by saving their emotions only for that God ordained person. Instruction on this point must be initiated at an early age before such emotional attachments begin. We need to tell children that God's standard is not that we just abstain from the physical. We must also hold back the emotional.

Parents need to instruct their children in the proper way to treat all members of the opposite sex **before** these emotional attachments begin. Train them to see others in the same way they would their natural siblings (1 Timothy 5:1-2). This would include treating them as a natural brother or sister not only physically but also emotionally. By encouraging them to guard their hearts, you will be helping to prevent them from giving pieces of themselves away in multiple relationships. You will be helping them to remain clear of memories they then will have to deal with once they are married. Going from one relationship to another is actually "divorce practice."

Some say this biblical approach to relationships is extreme. But what is truly extreme is the divorce rate, the suicide rate, the STD rate, the broken hearts, and the scarred and shattered lives. Don't base the use of God's standard on how you think your child will accept it; require it because it is His standard. Some parents will shy away from what is right only to teach what they think is acceptable. If you are firmly convinced of the biblical truth you will not fear the possibility of negative consequences, either from your child or society. Instead you will instruct out of a sense of genuine concern.

A word of caution before some of you go into this with your guns blazing: this may not the point upon which to begin your parenting. A parent must have already won the heart of their child, not just the fond affections. If a child is reluctant to receive instructions in lesser areas of proper conduct, it will be very difficult to require compliance in this area. The parent must work toward compliance in the lesser areas first to achieve compliance in this major one.

AVOIDING FOUR COMMON MISTAKES

WRONG STANDARD

There are four common mistakes many parents make, often unknowingly. The first is using their own life as the standard. Using unbiblical personal examples as the means of guiding a child is the leading cause of unbiblical training. Parents often excuse a child's wrongdoing by rationalizing, "I did that, and I'm OK." Whether your biased personal opinion of yourself is correct or not, you must acknowledge that we all have done things wrong in our past that despite them, thanks to God's grace, we can live a better life. Actions should be judged according to the Bible, not our opinion of ourselves and our life journey. Proverbs 17:13 says, *"If you call evil good, evil will never leave your house."*

A parent may consider something to be good because it brought them pleasure. If they have great memories of their opposite-sex relationships that were out of God's will, they may not see the dangers. Parents must be able to biblically look at their past and without reservation call sin, *sin*, without condemning themselves for a past they cannot change.

Vicarious Living

The second common mistake is training through vicarious living. Some parents wish they had been popular and had had a "great dating life." Out of regret, they encourage their children to have a lot of relationships, falsely thinking they are saving them from the same future regret. This is especially true concerning attendance at proms or other special events. The opposite is also true, when a parent has excitement over what they would consider "victories" or successes in dating. All such successes should be evaluated from a biblical perspective, not on the basis of emotional highs.

There is also the attitude, hidden deep within the heart, of wanting to relive the boyfriend/girlfriend hunting experience through their child. Parents have their children live out their fantasies, "If I can't date this person, the next best thing is for my child to do it."

Parents who still have sexually immoral beliefs place too much value on their child's appearance. Fathers who haven't dealt with their own sexual lust ultimately lead their own daughters into destructive behavior. Fathers may use those beliefs in an entirely different way than when they were single. When a daughter hears her father's prideful comments about her appearance to other people she is being told in essence what her value is. It is fine to privately compliment your child's appearance, but don't train any child to value appearance over character.

One father told me how excited he was about how his two daughters had become models. The way he told me was as if this was a greater success than if they had become brain surgeons. I don't want my daughters to be worshipped for their appearance.

I want them to be admired for their character and their service in the roles God asks of them.

Fear

A third common mistake parents make is by allowing parental fear to produce unbiblical solutions to parental concerns. Some parents fear their child will choose the wrong mate. In response they actually encourage their children to "date around" and explore all options before settling on the final one. This concept is based on the misconception that it is lack of "experience" that causes a person to make a poor mate choice. Such so-called "experience" is for the purpose of comparison shopping between marriage candidates to make sure they get the "best deal." This experience is considered by some people as a necessity if a wise and informed decision as to one's perfect mate is to be made.

This may sound like a good idea to some, but since when did entering into a romantic relationship cause people to think more clearly? (see Proverbs 30:18-19) If anything, a romantic relationship causes some to think less rather than more clearly. In fact, most people begin with blinders on and fail to see the true face of their romantic partner for some time. After watching their child's pain, a wise parent cannot help but to question the benefit of enduring several heartbreaks. Would not such painful experiences inevitably lead to emotional scars that can only harm any future relationship? And, even more importantly, how can dating around possibly be the right approach when it means the people involved are being unfaithful to their future spouse.

Other parents encourage dating around because they are afraid that their children will become too deeply attached to a person in their first romantic relationship. This fear can be affirmed because under our current culturally accepted dating practices the first person chosen for a romantic relationship doesn't have to meet any requirements for being a marriage partner; therefore, he/she isn't always a logical choice for marriage. Parents then fear their child will become overwhelmed by strong romantic emotions never experienced before, will mistake them for love, and be drawn into a marriage doomed for disaster. Their "solution" to this problem is to teach their child to move from one dating relationship to another quickly so that strong ties are not allowed to develop.

Although such parental fears are well-meaning, one must ask why anyone would want his child to enter a relationship if there is no intent to pursue it to the final step. Entering a romantic relationship for all sorts of reasons, whether it be for entertainment, or to sort through people looking for the "best" one, or purely for the physical pleasure merely places the person at risk of making a poor mate choice among other things. It just makes sense to never date someone you wouldn't or shouldn't marry. Also, it is wrong to toy with another person's strong emotions and then expect the relationship to come to a favorable end. Such cruelty often leads to tragedy.

Some parents who propose these and other unscriptural dating practices often are motivated by discontent. They may be unhappy with their marriage and wish he/she had kept looking and not "settled." For those who think that way, cleanse yourselves of your discontentment by honoring your spouse. If you don't, you will never have a great marriage and you will pass that discontent and lack of fulfillment along to your child through all sorts of unbiblical beliefs like the ones I just mentioned.

While it is appropriate for parents to not want their child to make incorrect mate choices, this is not how God intended parents to assist in the mate selection process. When parents propose this multiple relationship philosophy they are undermining His original design. What parents need to understand is that He intended the first romantic relationship to contain strong bonding emotions.

He created us that way because He never intended there to be more than one such relationship. What parents should be doing is instructing their children not to enter into a romantic relationship for any other purpose than a God-ordained relationship intended for marriage.

Self-esteem

The fourth common mistake parents make is using opposite-sex relationships to try to solve problems of low self-esteem. Teach your children they don't have to date to be special. They need to learn how to be content within themselves. This is so important! Your child is constantly being taught by society, media, and the comments adults make that we all need a boyfriend/girlfriend to be complete. Some children unwisely rest all of their hopes of building self-esteem by acquiring their "trophy" date. Parents think they can build their child's self-esteem by helping them to have a boyfriend or a girlfriend when in fact the opposite is true.

Children need to understand that it is right and healthy to trust His biblical plan of emotional and physical abstinence. If a person doesn't know that we all should be receiving our identity and having our need for love met by our heavenly Father then that person will look to other places to meet that need. Real self-esteem doesn't come from what other people think about you. It comes from knowing what God thinks about you. Perfect self-esteem lives independent of popular opinion. Parents often make the mistake of teaching their children how to fit in instead of how to stand alone.

Parents, when you teach your children the biblical standard of opposite-sex relationships, you are not only helping them prevent divorce, heartache, disease—even early death—you are also building a strong relationship with them. Every parent who wants to be involved in his/her children's lives as they grow to be adults, wants to have a positive impact on their future. When parents accept their God-given authority to protect and train their children, they are building a foundational relationship that one day will become a friendship. It is well worth every effort!

To summarize

- Parents, learn what the Bible has to say about opposite-sex relationships.
- Don't rely on your unbiblical personal examples.
- Encourage your children to remain emotionally faithful to a future spouse by saving all their romantic emotions for that person.
- Teach them the biblical method of choosing a mate.
- Help your child to make the commitment to wait for the specific person God has chosen just for them and support them as they travel that biblical path.

CHAPTER 3

THE TEST OF TRUTH

Need for Change

I hope by now that the need for change in the area of male/female relationships is obvious. It is sad to think that it has taken a divorce epidemic to bring many of us to that conclusion. Over the years I have paid careful attention to the resistance to the truth of what is necessary to make these changes. I needed to know what it was that caused people to shy away from the blessing of the truth found in God's Word—particularly since I had seen a miraculous near elimination of divorce among the people who were married in our single adult group.

My first thought about people's resistance to change is that it shouldn't take a rocket scientist to figure out what will happen if we don't make any changes. It amazes me when people want to defend what we are currently practicing in our male/female relationships, or when they want to make only slight changes. If we were slightly off track we could get by with slight changes, but we are not! We are *way* off track. I once saw a sign that read, "If you always do what you always did, you will always get what you always got." Other people have said that the definition of insanity is "doing the same thing expecting different results." Status-quo is not going to work in this situation. We must believe and act in a different manner to see a change in this dangerous trend.

Obstacle to Change

To have the greatest impact on this epidemic, it is crucial that people be willing to overcome their resistance to accepting the truth. To assist people in overcoming their resistance, we need to identify what the reasons are that are causing them to resist. The prerequisite to making this change is knowing **how** to rightly discern the truth. As with all truth found in God's Word, an essential requirement to accepting it is being willing to let go of anything contrary that we previously thought to be true. The only way to change is to let go of what is hindering you from that change, so you can hold onto what can help you.

It is important to always examine why we believe what we believe to see if it stands up to the test of truth. People use different ways to determine for themselves what is true. Thomas the apostle had his way, he wouldn't believe Jesus rose from the dead unless he saw Him with his own eyes (see John 20:26-28). He was probably accustomed to allowing his personal experience to be the determining factor of his beliefs. In response, Jesus told Thomas there was a better way of believing that has nothing to do with seeing or previous experiences (see verse 29). It is dangerous to have your beliefs so self-centered that life becomes all about "you". Hebrews 11:1 tells us: *"Now faith is the substance of things hoped for, the evidence of things not seen."* (NKJ) Have faith in what the Bible has to say about the subject, and thus make it all about Him.

In my next chapter I am going to share with you different methods people use to choose a mate. Before I do, I need to point out something to those of you who are already married who may be tempted to resist what I will be sharing. I want to make sure I don't lose you; you have a definite and important influence over what method people choose to use to find their mates.

One obstacle to this change is that people want to elevate their own personal example above scriptural directives as the basis for truth—particularly those who are already married. The temptation may be to judge the truth of this matter according to your personal romantic experiences. Your experience on an emotional issue such as this may be near and dear to your heart and your objectivity toward it can be easily lost. Please don't allow these experiences—whether positive or negative—to hinder you from receiving the biblical truth being taught here. Judge the accuracy of what I am saying by consultation with Scripture, not by your personal experience. If your personal experience was unbiblical, it does not hurt to admit that. That doesn't mean you are a bad person, nor does it mean that your relationship is automatically headed for divorce.

People have a tendency to think they are either one-hundred percent right or one-hundred percent wrong. In reality, we are all in-between most of the time. Those who hold to the 100 percent theory hate to admit they have done one thing wrong because in their minds it automatically puts them into the one-hundred per-cent wrong category.

Experience has value and can be useful for many things. Although it is not meant to establish truth, it can be used to illustrate truth where it applies. For example, some years ago there was a debate as to whether cigarette smoking was bad for one's health. Those who didn't believe there was a problem would often cite an example such as, "I know a man who smoked five packs a day and he lived till he was 105." Does that man's experience prove that smoking isn't bad for other human beings? Of course it doesn't; in fact, scientific research and testing has proven just the opposite.

So, just as a personal example cannot prove a point, so too should we not use a personal example to test a biblical truth. You will always find yourself in trouble when you try to adapt the truth to your life; rather you should be adapting your life to the truth.

One reason people want to elevate their personal experience above the Word of God is pride. Pride holds us prisoner to our imperfect past. Think of it this way: pride is the glue that sin sticks to. If you are already married and didn't use the biblical method, it may have been God's grace that allowed you to choose the right person despite using the wrong method. We often take way too much credit for the things that go right in our life, and give God too little praise and thanks for how He bypassed our actions and fulfilled His perfect plan.

Once the marriage vows have been taken, it is **irrelevant** whether the person selected is the right one or not; at that point, that person becomes the right one. God expects both parties to uphold the vows taken. Please do not misuse the Scripture verses and instruction meant for singles by applying them to someone who is married. This will only bring confusion to the issue, and our God is not the author of confusion!

A perfect example of this kind of misuse of Scripture can be found in the Church of Corinth. The people took the biblical truth that warns Christians about being unequally yoked with unbelievers and applied it to those who were already married. Unfortunately, this misapplication of a directive for singles caused some overzealous married believers to divorce their unbelieving mates. God surely didn't justify such behavior.

One problem with interpreting truth according to a person's own experience and making that as the standard is if someone did something one way and it was a success, is that level of success a standard we should all live by? Can one person's experience guarantee the same results for others? Is it possible that there is a better way? The answer is, of course, that God's way is always the better way. Experience is not the best teacher; the Holy Spirit is.

There are many books written about dating that use the authors' personal experiences as their basis for truth. The reason there are so many different books is there are so many different experiences. We cannot deny the experiences—they are real. However, we must determine which of those experiences are biblically based. Choose to use God's word as the authority, not someone's experience.

Following a biblical standard is important because it gives a predictable outcome. When we follow other people's unbiblical examples, we don't know where we will end up. On the other hand, biblical standards give us a way of measuring or comparing. We don't need to experiment with ideas to see if they will work; we have been given the sure word of prophecy (see 2 Peter 1:19). Never settle for any standard that is not biblical. Past performance is no guarantee of future results.

Cause and Effect

One way people try to justify their unscriptural beliefs as being the truth is by using this incorrect example of cause and effect. I know parents who believe that their way of parenting is correct based solely on how their child turned out. Such parents believe the only factor that led to their child's positive development was their influence, but in fact, there are many other factors that can be responsible. They have made an incorrect assumption based on the wrong cause for the effect. If that were the basis for truth about parenting, Mary and Joseph should be considered the greatest parents ever! They really did raise the son of God (unlike other parents who have only claimed to have done so).

Once Jesus used mud to put in a blind man's eyes to heal him. Was it the mud that caused the man to see? Can we conclude that all we need to do to see blind eyes open is to put mud in them? Did Jesus always use mud to heal the blind? The mud wasn't the cause of the cure. Care must be taken not to place our trust in the wrong cause of an effect.

I have heard advertisements about matchmaking clubs that credit their service for making a good match between a couple. The proof: the testimony of the couple who were married and really like being married. If those services were scripturally valid then everybody who used them would find marital bliss through them rather than the few who win the gamble.

Wrong Comparisons

Still another way people justify going against Scripture as the basis for truth is by using actions of other Christians as their standard. "I know a good Christian and he did it this way." Regardless of how "good" a Christian may be he/she is not the standard. If what is done follows a biblical standard then by all means follow that example, but do not suppose we have a blank check to do everything that person does. Christianity is not based on how Christians act, nor can it be rewritten by their actions. People can do a lot of things right, but not be correct in all of their actions.

Then there are people who try to justify what they believe to be true about relationships based upon an illustration that doesn't apply. It's the old inaccurate apples and oranges comparison. For example, they argue against the biblical teaching that it is not necessary to have a series of relationships in order to find the "perfect person" by comparing the process to a job search. They cite the fact that in a job search there is a necessity to make efforts that are exclusively for the purpose of finding that job, looking in the want ads, making phone calls, etc. The conclusion is, if you are looking for that perfect job you might have to have several jobs prior to finding the perfect one. Their belief is true for that illustration, but not for marriage. The only biblical comparison for a marriage relationship is Christ and the Church. Don't fall for any argument that will not stand up to this test.

Determine in your heart that you want to know what the Bible has to say about this subject. Don't allow anything or anyone's foolish arguments to keep you from the truth—even if it hurts. God gave us the Bible to guide us into all truth so we wouldn't be led astray. Put your trust in what the Bible has to say above all else as the basis for truth.

CHAPTER 4

GOD'S METHOD OF CHOOSING A MATE

Method is Important

I was stuck in traffic one day when I noticed a bumper sticker on the car ahead of me. It read: "ALL MEN ARE IDIOTS AND I MARRIED THEIR KING." I'm sure that woman meant to humorously indicate displeasure with her husband, but instead she revealed her own foolishness. After all, when she married King Idiot, she became Queen Idiot! The truth is that nobody made her marry the man—he was her choice!

We see here a person who was bitter over an unfulfilled dream of a successful marriage. What Queen Idiot would have us believe is that she is simply an innocent victim of her husband's wrong-doings; that the person she chose to marry was the source of her problems. In reality, the problem was not primarily **whom** she chose, but more importantly why she made that choice. What was the method she used to come to that decision?

The method one uses to choose a mate is not a trivial matter like choosing your favorite color. The choice of whom to marry is a very important choice and must be treated with extreme respect.

Therefore, the method of choosing a mate should also receive due respect. Currently it is rarely treated that way.

The choice of whom to marry has a far-reaching impact on one's life. Marriage affects and often determines many of the beliefs and values a person has. The choice will also determine if one or both of the people in the relationship will fulfill much of God's plan for his or her life. It will also affect the lives of future children and, in the long run, help to define society's beliefs and values.

God indicated the seriousness of this choice during the days of Noah. At that time, mankind was so wicked God was grieved He had created them. What is interesting is that what is mentioned in Genesis, chapter 6, prior to God saying He would send the flood, is not a list of sins we would typically expect, but rather that people were marrying anybody they chose. Marriage was then, as it is many times today, merely a social event lacking God's influence.

When seeking a mate, people tend to concentrate more on getting who they "think" is the right person than on using the right method. But the method used to choose a marriage partner is equally, if not more, important than the person someone chooses. Choosing the right person, but using the wrong method, will cause problems. On the other hand, if the biblically-based method is followed, one is guaranteed to find the specific person God has ordained for them. The journey in this most important facet of life is just as important as the destination. I am not asking those of you who are not married to choose a person to marry right now, but you should choose the method you will use to select that person.

Some singles unintentionally have already chosen their method. Those who have, in most cases, are using a flawed method. Why? God's method does not come naturally, it must be learned. *"That each one of you <u>know how to take a wife</u> for himself in holiness and honor, not in the passion of lust like heathen who do not know God"* (1 Thes. 4:4-5 RSV). This verse does not say that each of you already knows this, it implies that the knowledge has to be learned. If it is not learned, then the consequences of not following the tenets of this verse should be expected.

This verse in Thessalonians speaks of two different and opposite ways to choose a wife. One method is based on holiness and shows honor; the other is based on lust as is usual in those who don't know God. Christians should approach choosing a mate in a totally different manner than that of those of the world. That is not my opinion; it is what the Bible says.

After studying different methods people use to choose a mate, I was able to lump them into one of three categories. I titled them Revelation, Resume, and Forfeit. *Revelation* is where God reveals to a person whom he/she is to marry. *Resume* is where someone decides whom he or she will marry based only on information about them, and then informs God of their choice. *Forfeit* is where sin pressures someone into marrying. *Out of the three basic methods of choosing a mate, only one is biblically based and thus contributes mightily to the success of the marriage.* This biblical principle of how to choose a mate has more of a dramatic effect on the beliefs and behaviors of those who are single than any other principle about being single I know. So let's begin with the best method—Revelation. I will cover the other two in the next chapter.

Specific Plan

The Revelation Method is based on the fact that God has a specific plan for each of our lives. *"All the days ordained for me were written in your book before one of them came to be"* (Ps 139:16). Prior to your first day of conception, God ordained each following day of your life's journey. The Bible also says *"Before I formed you in the womb I knew you, before you were born I set you apart"* (Jer. 1:5). Before you were born, God gave you gifts and talents in order to fulfill His plan and purpose in your life. His perfect plan is what makes you a unique, precious, and valuable person. Respecting that plan is a must for those who want to please Him.

The plan God has for your life is specific. *"God determined the times set for us and the exact places where we should live"* (Acts 17:26). Just as He set out time and place for the early Christians, He does so for us today. It is no coincidence when and where you were born; God is a specific God. *"The steps of a good man are ordered by the LORD"* (Ps. 37:23 KJV). That's a lot of steps! *"For we are God's workmanship, created in Christ Jesus **to do good works**, which God prepared **in advance** for us to do"* (Eph 2:10).

There are some general instructions written in the Bible that apply to everyone, but the specific plan is not written in any book anywhere. The only way we can find that plan is by asking God, and that fact makes us totally dependent on Him. We have to get away from any philosophy that tries to create independence from God. *"Let us throw off everything that hinders and the sin that so easily entangles, and let us run with perseverance **the race marked out for us**"* (Heb 12:1). Your race is different than my race; my race is different than yours. The Bible addresses many issues that are common to every person, but each of us has a specific race that is unique to him or her.

Knowing that there is a plan makes us want to seek and reach out for God to find out what that special plan is. *"He determined the times set for them and the exact places where they should live. God did this **so that** men would **seek** him and perhaps **reach out for** him and find him, though he is not far from each one of us"* (Acts 17:26-27). Knowing that God has a specific plan for your life changes everything from just following rules to your needing a relationship with Him.

Some incorrectly view God's plan for this life as being whatever good and bad things that happen to them. We should never passively interpret God's plan for our life by our circumstances. God's plan entails the calling and purpose for your life—your God given assignments to accomplish on this earth. The negative things that happen in life are obstacles to the fulfilling of the assignments

God gives you. He definitely uses those negative things and makes positive things out of them, but He is not the cause of them.

Following God's plan also restricts our options; we shouldn't be doing just anything that appeals to us. Proverbs 29:18 tells us *"where there is no revelation, the people cast off restraint."* Jesus didn't do whatever he wanted to; He restricted his life by only doing the will of the Father. John 5:19 says, *"The Son can do nothing by himself; he can do only what he sees his Father doing."* And, in Ephesians 4:11 it says, *"God gave some to be apostles, some to be prophets, some to be evangelists, and some to be pastors and teachers."* It does not say God asks who wants to be an apostle or pastor. God has never approached someone and said, "I have a lot of work that needs to be done. Here is a list of things that need to be done so take your pick of what you would like to do." God is always specific.

One Specific Person

God's specific plan includes a specific person to marry for those called to marriage. Because His plan is so specific, it would be foolish to believe that it doesn't include the person we should marry, particularly because this choice has such a major effect on our ability to follow God's plan in other areas of life. It seems odd to me that some people believe God has a specific job He wants them at right now, and a specific Church He wants them to attend, yet when it comes to something even more important, such as choosing a mate, they believe there isn't one specific choice. I believe the Bible indicates that God does have a specific person for one to marry. I base this on Genesis 2:21: *"So the LORD God caused the man to fall into a deep sleep; and while he was sleeping, he took one of the man's ribs and closed up the place with flesh."* God took only one rib from Adam to make his one mate, thereby indicating just how specific that person is. He could have easily taken a half dozen ribs and made a half dozen women and allowed Adam to pick his favorite. But He didn't, and for good reason—His choice fits into His perfect plan.

Don't use the legalistic view of one rib. What happens if someone's spouse dies? Have they used up their one specific person? No! God is more concerned with the reason for the principle than He is the rule of the principle.

I have never heard scriptural evidence to prove that God doesn't have a specific person He intends for someone to marry, but I have heard some situational examples that people use to dispute this belief. The basic problem with those examples is they never take into account the power of God; instead, they play on people's fear. Some examples would be, "Out of the five billion people on this planet, how could there be only one person" or, "What if the one person gets hit by lightning?"

There is no doubt in my mind that God is more than capable of locating two people in the midst of a crowd of five billion and bringing those two together. He also knows what is to happen from the beginning to the end of each life here on earth and thus would know that this specific person would get hit by lightning. God plans according to foreknowledge. *"For those God foreknew he also predestined to be conformed to the likeness of his Son, that he might be the firstborn among many brothers"* (Rom. 8:29). [That subject's for another time and place. Don't get caught up in trying to over-intellectualize this truth.]

It's Who They Are

The Revelation Method is driven by **who** the special person is. In Genesis 2:21-23 God reveals to Adam who he is to marry. *"So the LORD God caused **the man** to fall into a deep sleep; and while he was sleeping, he took **one** of **the man's** ribs and closed up the place with flesh. Then the LORD God made a woman from the rib he had taken out of **the man**, and he brought **her** to **the man**"* (v.21-22).

After God puts Adam to sleep and takes **one** of his ribs. He then forms Eve from that rib. Then He brings Eve to Adam, which indicates to us that He hadn't formed Eve in Adam's presence. But, immediately, Adam recognizes her as his rib. Verse twenty-three: *"The man said, "This is now bone of my bones and flesh of my flesh; she shall be called 'woman,' for she was taken out of man."* In modern vernacular, Adam's first response to seeing Eve was, "Hey, this is the rib that was taken out of me." That's what a rib is, flesh and bone. Adam's first response wasn't to evaluate Eve to see if she was his type or if he liked her or not. Adam's response was to **who** Eve was in **relationship** to him, not any attribute about her. That goes beyond any likes or dislikes of a person. Her relationship to him was she was flesh of his flesh and bones of his bones. This is what set her apart from all of creation. Eve was related to Adam the same way a parent is to a child. Since a child is a reproduction of the parent's flesh and bones, the parent/child relationship is based on who the person is and not on what the other person can do for them.

The question then arises, how did he know **she** was his rib? She didn't look anything like a rib and he wasn't there when God formed her. So, the only way for Adam to know Eve was his rib was for God to reveal that information to him. The Revelation Method is based on the biblical truth of what happened here in Genesis. God revealed that Eve was part of Adam.

That is how the first marriage originated, but God's pattern for marriage did not end there. As we read further we find: *"For this reason a man will leave his father and mother and be united to his wife, and they will become one flesh"* (Gen. 2:24). Up to this point in Scripture, all references to Adam were written as **the man**; in fact, nine times Adam is referred to in this manner. Now, for the very first time, there is a reference to **a man**, so the reference is not referring to Adam. Who, then, is Genesis 2:24 referring to? It is referring to people who have a father and mother. Adam and Eve didn't have a natural father and mother. They were created by the Father. So, this Scripture is speaking to everyone after them; to those of us who have a human father and mother.

The Revelation Method is as relevant today as it was back then. Jesus referred to it in Matthew, chapter nineteen, when He was responding to a question about the problem of divorce.

> *"Some Pharisees came to him to test him. They asked, "Is it lawful for a man to divorce his wife for any and every reason?"*
>
> *"Haven't you read,"* he replied, [didn't you read the Bible] *that at the beginning* [talking about Genesis] *the Creator 'made them male and female,'* [He's referring to Genesis 1:27] *and said, 'For this reason a man will leave his father and mother and be united to his wife, and the two will become one flesh'?*
> —Quoting Genesis 2:24; Matt 19:3-5

This "one flesh" concept is also used in Ephesians 5:28-32 when discussing how a husband should relate to a wife.

One Specific Reason to Marry

According to the Bible, there is **one specific reason** that should lead a person to decide to get married. *"For this reason a man will leave his father and mother and be united to his wife, and they will become one flesh"* (Gen. 2:24). The subject of this verse is marriage but it begins by saying *for this reason*. What reason is this verse talking about? It is the reason that is mentioned in verses twenty-one through twenty-three which tell us that God has revealed to a person who their mate is. In other words, *The reason someone should get married is because God has revealed to them a specific person to marry*. This should be the basis for deciding to marry. Unfortunately, today we see people getting married for all sorts of reasons. "I had this feeling that just wouldn't go away." "She was so attractive." "He made me feel special." These are all secondary to the biblical reason found in Genesis 2:24.

How the Revelation Comes

Now that we know God uses the Revelation Method, the next thing we have to know is how He makes us aware of this revelation. The answer is found in Psalm 37:4 and John 14:7: this instructs us how God directs a person's desires. *"Delight yourself in the LORD and he will give you the desires of your heart"* (Ps 37:4). This does not mean that God will give us whatever we desire. But if we are delighting in Him, He will give us **what** we should desire and in the case of marriage, **whom** we should desire. Jesus said, *"If you remain in me and my words remain in you, ask whatever you wish, and it will be given you"* (John 14:7). Again, this is not saying that God will give us whatever we want. It is saying that if we remain in Jesus and His words remain in us we would never ask for just anything. We would only ask for those things God would want us to ask for.

Some are unable to grasp the simplicity of receiving revelation from God through our desires because they are looking for something different. They think God **only** works through the spectacular, but He is never limited to that. He doesn't have to audibly tell someone or write the message in the sky. The desire that God gives someone is similar to other desires. The urge to indulge in ice cream is a desire, the urge to buy a new car is a desire. But the difference between the desire God gives and the desire for ice cream lies in where it came from. One desire comes from seeing a Dairy Queen; the other comes from God.

Therefore, it becomes important to be able to distinguish between our self-created desires and God-sent desires. We have been created with free will; subsequently, we can create our own desires apart from God. We can create desire by giving someone or something time and attention. In theory, you can "fall in love" with a fence post if you give it enough time and attention! Therefore, since it is possible to create your own desires, it is essential to take precautions to stay away from outside influences that would create desires apart from God in the area of choosing a mate.

It takes physical and emotional abstinence to actually receive God's desires, and not create a desire for someone apart from God's plan. The Bible tells us how to remain physically and emotionally pure as we wait for God's revelation: *"Treat younger women as sisters, with absolute purity"* (1 Tim 5:2). The Phillips translation says to *"Treat them as younger sisters with purity and no more."* By treating **all** members of the opposite sex the way we would treat a natural brother or sister, one is able to remain physically and emotionally pure without creating desires that stem from the physical and not from God's leading. *"I made a covenant with my eyes not to look lustfully at a girl,"* Job cries in 31:1. Then, in Proverbs 4:23, we find *"guard your heart."* All of these Scriptures advise that a person should neither give special time nor attention to a person they will never marry.

Revelation Provides Faith

True revelation is not just the knowledge of something, it becomes an inseparable part of a person. Revelation provides faith. When the going gets tough, revelation knowledge provides an anchor for your soul. It is a strong fortress against the storms of life. Once a person is truly convinced the mate he/she has chosen is in God's will, that decision will never have to be doubted or questioned. He/she will be sure that this person is the only mate, rather than thinking the person is merely one of many possibilities. Only the Revelation Method contributes to long-term success of a marriage. Even though it's been almost twenty years since the Lord revealed who my wife was, that revelation is still a source of strength for me today. Even if we travel through rough seas, I never have to wonder if I made a mistake.

The revelation of who someone's mate is needs to come to both persons involved. It is not enough for one person to receive the revelation; both parties are entitled to receive the benefit of their own revelation. Whoever receives the revelation first should not disclose the news to the future mate until that person has also received their personal revelation from God. There must not be any undue influence or pressure placed on the other person. True love will not want to steal the beauty of this comforting assurance coming directly from the Father.

Of course, the next question is, how does someone know when the other person has their revelation, since the two parties are not supposed to tell each other? My answer: They must use the same God-given patience that got them to this point. They must not let go of that patience because of the excitement and expectations they are now facing due to this future relationship. As for how they know when the other person knows, this is another job for God. He will let them know when the time is right. As you see, everything I am telling you about the way the Revelation Method works forces the person to be dependent on God, and that is a very good thing!

Early Commitment

The earlier in life the Revelation Method is chosen, the better. The earlier one uses emotional and physical abstinence, the more protection it provides—not only against the creation of wrong desires, but also against unfaithfulness to one's future spouse. This is where parents can play a vital part in their child's life by teaching and encouraging this method. Faithfulness to a mate should begin long before God reveals who that mate will be. The fact that someone hasn't met their mate yet should not be an excuse for the person to be unfaithful or to behave differently than if their special person were already physically present to oversee their behavior. Many people pretend their mate doesn't exist, merely because they don't know who they are. And, since they don't believe the unknown mate is watching, they reason, "How could that person ever know." The truth is if God has marriage in His perfect plan for you, your specific mate does exist and all actions do matter.

I believe the strength of a decision is in the length of that decision. To commit to loving a person for five minutes is easy. To commit to loving a person for the rest of your life after you meet them is a strong commitment. But when you commit to loving a person before that person is met and for the rest of your life you have made the strongest commitment one can make to a relationship. It is a testimony of the degree of commitment you will bring to your future spouse.

Let's look at this relationship commitment from the other person's perspective. If you were them what would you want your future mate to be doing? Would you want them to be faithful to you and not be in any relationships with other people? Would you want them to be emotionally and physically abstinent? If that is what you would want from them, then that's what you should also be doing. Matthew 7:12 says it best: *"So in everything, do to others what you would have them do to you, for this sums up the Law and the Prophets."*

What should happen after both parties receive their revelation and they both know that? It must be time to announce the engagement and plan the wedding, right? Warning! It's time to slow down, not speed ahead. Some have unwisely mistaken God's revelation of their mate as permission to get married immediately. Knowing whom to marry is just the beginning; there is a lot more work ahead in learning how to relate to one another. If you skip the time needed to develop a great relationship prior to marriage you will set yourselves up for a lot of unnecessary problems. Skipping a stage or speeding one up is like building a house with the walls and roof, and then having to go back to build the foundation.

At times God reveals who a mate is, but He does not intend that the couple go beyond a brother/sister relationship at that time. They might be unequally yoked at that time, or one or both may be spiritually immature or a recent convert. God always has reasons for his actions. He times every aspect of the relationship. And His timing should be followed not only for when the couple should cross over the brother/sister relationship into a pre-marriage relationship, but also for when the wedding ceremony should take place. Remember, there is not only an appointed person but also appointed times for each stage of the developing relationship.

A good example of this is a young man who led a young woman to the Lord and she began to attend his Church. God showed him he would eventually marry her. Most young men would make a mistake at this time and rush to get immediately involved in a romantic relationship. Instead this man took the hands-off approach and allowed other women in the Church to disciple his future mate. This gave her an opportunity to grow in the Lord without the added pressure of being in a relationship leading to marriage

One of the reasons people believe it is all right to speed ahead is because they think being God's specific person means they are also a perfect person. I am careful to always refer to the mate God has for someone as the "specific" person and not the "perfect" person. There are no perfect people. Many people are disillusioned to believe in this concept and it has produced disastrous results. Adam was the first to have such a belief. He thought Eve was perfect because God gave her to him. Remember, everything God had given Adam up to that point was perfect. As a result he became mad at God and blamed Him for his disobedience to Him because "the woman" He gave him wasn't perfect.

Listening to God and hearing His voice in all areas of life is important. Unfortunately many people have made mistakes in presuming they have heard from God who their mate is. This is definitely an area in which someone doesn't want to make a mistake. Therefore, it's important to have experience in hearing God's voice in regard to smaller and less important issues first. This is where following biblical singleness really pays off (topic covered in a later chapter). *Time is your friend.* The worst thing you can do is rush. After all, the first thing mentioned about love in 1 Corinthians 13:4 is that love is patient!

I have seen plenty of abuses in the use of the Revelation Method, where people tell me, "I think I have heard from God." Sometimes it is a true accident, but other times it is just wishful thinking. The worst case scenario occurs when someone is trying to manipulate another person with his or her "revelation" by telling them, "God told me we should get married and if you don't agree with that you're not spiritual." As with anything that is true, there is always a segment of the society who will misuse the method or do it incorrectly. Subsequently, *abuses should never be used to invalidate the Revelation Method.*

I know different authors who disagree with these principles just because of the problems caused by people's misuse. I too am grieved by such flakiness and misuse. Let me assure you it is completely within the character of God to allow us to have something that can be misused. He has gifted us all with free will. His intent in doing so is we could freely love Him. On the other hand, free will is also the reason we have every problem in the world today. We likewise don't reject the idea of grace just because somebody uses it for the wrong purpose. The Apostle Paul warned of such misuse in Romans 6:1-2.

Let me also say something about the authors with whom I disagree on this one point—I still can respect and agree with the other principles they teach and I do not reject them or their work just because of this one point of disagreement. Regardless of controversy, we should stand for the biblical principles that are found in the Revelation Method and see their value in creating strong marriages and in solving the divorce epidemic.

Regardless of whom someone chooses to marry, there is always a process or method used to make that choice. The method chosen will contribute either to the success or the failure of the marriage. So let's concentrate on preventing problems after marriage by emphasizing what can be done before marriage to help reduce problems later on. One of the most effective ways to do this is to follow God's method of choosing a mate.

CHAPTER 5

MAN-MADE METHODS OF CHOOSING A MATE

God's Wisdom vs Man's

God's wisdom is always immeasurably superior to ours. Whenever He gives us instructions on a subject, and we decide to follow another path, we are headed toward trouble. By choosing to rely upon our own wisdom instead of God's, we are implying we know better than He does—that, for some reason, God hasn't given us the best instructions and there is room for us to improve upon them. Such is the case with choosing a mate. There can be only one, God-ordained method for choosing a mate; any other method comes strictly from man-made wisdom. Believing in a different method other than the one that God has given us is always an inferior belief. We have already discussed God's method, so let's take a look at the man-made methods popular at this time. It was important to cover the best method first so that as we look at the other methods, and compare them to God's idea; we can see just how foolish they are in comparison. Most of the principles that surround the methods designed by man fall into one of two categories. I call them resume and forfeit.

Resume Method

The Resume Method consists of a list of mate qualifications that reflect what that person believes will make him or her happy. This "I want" list can be either written or unwritten.

The resume list contains requirements, such as a certain type of personality or hobbies. It may also have some over-emphasized requirements such as high social and economic status. Many contain some excellent standards such as positive character qualities. Unfortunately, much too often there is an emphasis on outward appearance. Some Christians in an effort to "fool" God about how important appearance is to them will place such items on the bottom of their list. They're not fooling anyone, only themselves. 1 Samuel 16:7 tells us that *"The LORD does not look at the things man looks at. Man looks at the outward appearance, but the LORD looks at the heart"* (NIV).

One of the inherent problems with the list-matching Resume Method lies with the author of the list. People who use this method rely solely on his or her own intellect and/or senses to engineer a relationship. Proverbs 3:5 specifically tells us not to do that. It is prideful to think that, in comparison to God, any one of us is smart enough to know how to meet our own needs.

In the Resume Method, mate selection is based upon a person earning that position. With the list of qualifications doing the leading, the selection is not based on who the other person is, but rather on what that person can do. The selection process is performance based and those who use it falsely believe that God's guidance is unnecessary. They only call on Him if and when they can't get the person they want. What they don't realize is God isn't obligated to get anyone the marriage partner of their choosing.

I have seen people become so dependant on their self created list that when God did bring the specific person into their life they agonized over the fact if they were the one or not because there was one minor thing on their list that person didn't fulfill. The list became more of a distraction rather than a help.

At first, using a self-created list may not seem like a bad idea, until one compares it to the belief that God has a specific person for those who marry. In Genesis, chapter twenty-five, we find that God's plan for Esau's life was for him to be the oldest son of Jacob. But Esau despised his birthright. The sin of Esau was in his believing there was something more important in his life than God's plan for him (see Genesis 25:29-34). Esau was self-ruled and indiscriminate about his life choices, which is basically called godlessness. The Bible shows us similarities between being godless and being sexually immoral. *"See that no one is sexually immoral, or is godless like Esau, who for a single meal sold his inheritance rights as the oldest son"* (Hebrews 12:16). Unlike Esau, you should cherish God's plan for your life and never trivialize it.

The main problem with the list idea is that it is just not specific enough. You are making a major life decision based upon a comparatively limited amount of information. *The list is so general, more than one person can match it.* The most important piece of information that is missing from such a list is God's master plan for each person's life. Because the Resume Method is not specific enough it creates instability, and confusion because there is always that nagging thought in the back of your mind, "Maybe there's someone else with a better resume that I just haven't met yet."

If I were to write a list of the character and personality traits, likes and dislikes of my wife, and anonymously make the list public, the chances of anyone finding her from that list would be extremely slim. Yet, that is what some people expect the Resume Method to do for them. It is a real gamble at best to find a specific person that way.

Let's compare the Resume method to the scriptural model God gives us in Genesis chapter two. If He had wanted us to use the resume method to find our mate, Adam would have asked Eve when

God brought her to him, do you like to ski, what is your favorite restaurant? Adam didn't have a list. He accepted the mate God provided for him. People get married because they have common interests like golf for example, but when they get divorce they still have that common interest, it is just that common interests are not able to keep people together. On the other hand, if we maintain the proper relationship to that person it is sufficient to provide a lifetime relationship.

So, why do some people seek a mate through the list method? Many use the list as protection against their fear that God's choice might not be a good one. Those who don't really trust God, or don't know Him well, think He might be intentionally cruel and make someone marry an "ugly" person. What they don't seem to understand is that when people trust God to give them the desires of their heart that also includes the desire for that future mate's appearance. Once again, this is not that God provides the mate who matches whatever physical appearance someone has previously developed an appetite for while comparison shopping; rather, God provides the desire for whatever the specific person looks like. God would never have you marry someone to whom you were not physically attracted. You *can* trust Him in this area! He created you and this mate matching plan. He knows exactly how it should work. If you can't trust the Creator, who can you trust?

Filling the List

Once a person has his or her shopping list in hand, he/she then feels the need to search for someone to match that list. To find out if someone matches the list, it is necessary to gather information about them. Thus dating becomes an interviewing process. The seeker wanders in and out of different relationships to either "find" the person who fits the list, or to figure out what else to put on the list. Such multiple relationships make excellent divorce practice, but then, why would anyone want to practice that!

The Resume Method usually involves comparing one person to another. Relationships are formed for the **purpose** of comparing. "I like this person better than the last person, but I still wish I could find someone like the person three relationships ago." The problem is, the habit of making comparisons doesn't go away when someone gets married. Comparing one person to another creates two problems—unfaithfulness and discontent. Unfaithfulness occurs because in order to decide what characteristics you would like your future mate to have, you must think of each person you date in a way that should be reserved for your spouse. That type of thinking should be reserved for only one specific person. One of the major causes of discontentment in a marriage is often caused by the devaluation of one's spouse because he or she is not like somebody else.

Another byproduct of comparison thinking is rejection. If someone is not able to fit your resume, they are rejected as being inferior. This is not true under God's Revelation Method, because those decisions are not based on someone's opinion of an individual. The person is either part of God's plan for their life or they're not—it's nothing personal.

Some think they have bypassed all that is wrong with this process by using a dating service by allowing someone else assist them with their sorting. Unfortunately, dating services operate on the Resume Method. I don't believe any dating service is truly Christian; it's the same as having a "Christian bar"—it just doesn't make sense when the approach is contrary to God's plan. These services attempt to engineer a relationship based on matching items on two lists. The assumption is, if you have this certain type of a person then this other type of person would be the "perfect match" for them-as long as this "perfect" person is a paying customer that is. The standard used to determine which two types of people will fit together is flawed because it is determined by the dating service, not God. And once again, the main "match" is missing. The dating service doesn't know God's plan for each person's life!

Is it possible for two people to meet through a dating service and be God ordained for each other? Absolutely! Should we give the credit to the dating service? No way! Once again, God's mercy has stepped in and bypassed his and her actions.

Of course, not everything about the list idea is bad. Character qualifications and standards play a major part in every relationship. I'm not saying that a person shouldn't have a list of good character qualities he or she desires in a mate; the question is what is that list being used for? The point to keep in mind is that the list is not to be used to determine who someone's mate is. Do parents love their children based on their character qualities or how "cute" they are? Do they get rid of older children and get new ones when the old ones don't meet expectations? Of course not! And yet this is what our menu driven society has produced: drive-thru marriages and disposable relationships.

There is a mass of good information in print today about relationships. The problem is that this information is being used for the wrong purpose. It should not be used to find a mate; its purpose is to improve a relationship after God has brought two people together. Once God has revealed the specific mate, then character qualifications can be used to determine at what **level** the relationship should begin. Finding character flaws doesn't mean that the God-ordained relationship should end. If one of the people in the relationship is struggling in certain areas, or is not ready for marriage, then the relationship goes no further than brother/sister at this time. This just means the couple takes time to develop a best-friend scenario and maturely work things out. They can now seek godly counsel from someone who has a biblical understanding of relationships, and thus sets a pattern for their future marriage.

In the world, instead of learning how to work things out and—"oh, no! do I have to?"—change, it's easier to move on to the next relationship or get a divorce. But in God's perfect plan, the couple shouldn't even think of a wedding, or for that matter an engagement, if there are unresolved character and spiritual maturity issues. *"How can two walk together unless they be agreed"* (Amos 3:3). There are no perfect people. Those who are single should concentrate on marrying the **specific** person God has selected for them, and while waiting they should prepare for that marriage before it is entered into.

The Forfeit Method

A second alternative of improperly choosing a mate is the Forfeit Method. In this method, the person gives control to someone or something other than to God or logic. The Forfeit Method has all the traits of an addiction—a **seemingly** irresistible impulse to act irrationally, thus forcing bad judgment. This mindless method allows emotions or physical pleasure to force someone into a particular mate choice.

You may have wondered why two particular people ever made the choice to marry each other. What could they possibly have been thinking? Actually, they weren't thinking. They lost control when they gave place in their life to something other than God.

Some people believe they have no control over who they "fall in love" with. Let me assure you, you don't fall in love! You fall in a pit or a hole, or into sin, but not in love. [More about this in a later chapter.] So-called love that is "fallen into" often comes as a result of not physically and/or emotionally abstaining, so "love" becomes a self-created desire not one ordained or given by God. A desire for someone, either good or bad, can happen in an instant, but by itself it is not love. God doesn't want people to be trapped or deceived into marriage.

Some people look at a person across the room and think they have found love. They don't even know if the person they are looking at can speak the same language, but their eyes meet and it's all over but the wedding bells. This is the epitome of the Forfeit Method of mate choice.

The most common way of forfeiting choice is by entering into a relationship before someone truly hears from God as to whether the other person is **the** person. They enter into a relationship to see if they are interested in choosing that person; then, after they decide, they ask God His opinion. The problem is that God didn't initiate the relationship, He was being asked about it after the fact. I have seen many singles struggle as they question if the person they are currently in a relationship with is the one or not. Often, the claim is, "I can't hear from God" when in fact the problem is they don't want to hear that the person they have chosen is not the one. A conflict is created because the pull of emotional ties to someone can be so strong that it makes it difficult to hear from God. The agony and the error that comes from choosing your mate that way can be devastating.

The Forfeit Method is promoted by some by using the false reasoning that someone will never get married if he or she doesn't date around. The reason this appears to work is that sooner or later they will get addicted to someone. Sadly, the someone isn't necessarily the specific person, or even a logical choice.

People do not directly decide to forfeit, it comes as a by-product of certain beliefs and behaviors. Forfeiting isn't the result of an intellectual deficiency. This is not just a matter of poor judgment; it's clouded judgment. There are specific beliefs and behaviors that have an intoxifying effect that impair judgment and make us susceptible to poor judgment. God tells us to stay away from those beliefs and behaviors that force us into giving up sound judgment.

The prospect of the pleasure of sexual immorality is a lure into otherwise unjustifiable actions. The purpose of a lure is to cause a behavior that would otherwise not happen. A fish would be highly unlikely to jump on a hook without some kind of bait to deceive it into doing so. If it wasn't for the prospect of pleasure from an immoral act, many actions would be unthinkable. Proverbs 11:22 warns: *"Like a gold ring in a pig's snout is a beautiful woman who shows no discretion."* The patterns of this world train us to focus on the gold ring, and ignore the pig behind it.

Sexual lust is one of the most powerful drives in human beings. Professionals have damaged their reputations and bankrupted themselves both financially and spiritually because of their inability to conquer it. Some men have risked imprisonment or death to sate the intense urge. It is probably the greatest factor in mate selection that causes future regret. Often the people who use the Forfeit Method to find a mate become bitter and cynical because they realize after the wedding what a dumb thing they did. Although the sexual urge wants to control us, through Christ we can master it.

Forfeiting may also come as the result of a lifestyle and not just one behavior. Ephesians 4:17-24 tells us that those who live apart from God have their understanding darkened, and they separate themselves from the life of God because of the hardening of their hearts. If someone conforms to the principles of this world he or she will not be able to discern what God's will is. *"Do not conform any longer to the pattern of this world, but be transformed by the renewing of your mind.* **Then** *[And only then] you will be able to test and approve what God's will is—his good, pleasing and perfect will"* (Rom. 12:2). The patterns of this world steal our ability to discern God's will. The deception makes us believe we know what God's will is when we really don't.

Jonah 2:8 tells us that *"Those who cling to worthless idols forfeit the grace that could be theirs."* Idols are things that are more important to someone than God is. God wants to give us grace, but those who hang onto an idol forfeit that grace by giving someone or something a higher position in their life than they do God.

The Bible tells us that **our own desires can betray us**. *"You were taught, with regard to your former way of life, to put off your old self,* *which is being corrupted by its **deceitful desires***" [or in the Weymouth translation "*misleading impulses*"] (Eph 4:22). Remember Queen Idiot? The reason she wasn't thrilled with her mate choice was most likely because she had become a victim of her own misleading impulses. Being desperate and lonely is no condition from which to choose a mate. The timing is worse than going to the grocery store hungry and the results more devastating. The Bible also tells us we can be controlled by our sinful nature when we live according to sensuality.

> *"Those who live according to the sinful nature have their minds set on what that nature desires; but those who live in accordance with the Spirit have their minds set on what the Spirit desires. The mind of sinful man is death, but the mind controlled by the Spirit is life and peace; the sinful mind is hostile to God. It does not submit to God's law, nor can it do so. Those **controlled** by the sinful nature cannot please God."*
>
> —Rom. 8:5-8

First Timothy 5:11 talks about people who allow their sensuality to overcome their dedication to Christ. When we lose our dedication to Christ we end up being controlled by negative influences. If pleasure becomes more important to someone than virtue, problems inevitably occur. God is not against pleasure; He just understands its adverse effects when it becomes too high a priority. He doesn't tell us that sex outside of marriage is forbidden merely because He wants to test people to see if they can control themselves. He tells us that fornication is a sin because He understands the problems that arise from sex outside of marriage. In His love, He tries to protect us from harming ourselves or others. Pleasing God is always in our best interest and for our own protection. It is our dedication to Christ that keeps us from being controlled by negative influences.

To those of you who are single and have chosen to incorporate the Resume or Forfeit Method of finding a mate into your lifestyle, I encourage you to reconsider. Choose God's Revelation Method. It is the only one that contributes to the success of a marriage. There is nothing better than doing things God's way. It's when we do things our own way that we end up miserable and discontented. If you haven't used the Revelation Method before, you can start now. Even if you have been doing things the wrong way, God is ready and able to help you change. "His mercies are new every morning…"

CHAPTER 6

FINDING VS. SEARCHING FOR A MATE

Although this chapter describes what biblical actions older adult children should be participating in, the knowledge of this needs to be shared with parents of all ages. Parents of younger children need an overview of the entire biblical marriage process to let them know what they should be preparing their child for. Parents always need to look to the future to determine what beliefs are beneficial in creating a positive future.

The Need to Locate a Mate

Many believe all that keeps a single person from getting the relationship started that will eventually lead to marriage is that they just haven't **found** the right person yet. They believe that all that separates them from their future mate is being at the same location at the same time. Therefore, it becomes necessary to run from one place to another in order to cross paths with that other person. After all, "if they don't search for them how will they meet them?"

If this is all that stands in the way, then why not spend every waking moment searching? Try to cover as much ground as possible, scour the land. Figure out a strategy of where the best target spots are, and then follow it. The search must always be on! God's timing has nothing to do with it.

One of the difficulties with this approach is that not only does a person have to cover all the targeted territory, he/she also has to be at the right location at the right time. This means the searcher cannot go to several locations just once, he/she has to revisit those same locations because the special person they are looking for might not have been there at the same time. What makes this even more difficult is that when the other person in this potential relationship is also searching it now becomes more difficult to hit the moving target. It's like playing telephone tag.

The next problem is that once these two people get to the right place at the right time, how do they recognize each other? Chances are they won't have a yellow sticky note on their forehead indicating "Here I am!" So the searchers are always asking themselves, "Is this the one, or not?" They are always wondering "what if," always enlisting potential candidates. Which person is it that has the ability to discern which two people should be together and where they are located? Wouldn't it make more sense to set a time and place to meet? God has done just that; He has set both the right time and place.

Those who are single often get themselves in trouble because they don't know whose responsibility it is to bring them and their future mate together. They often make this a more complicated task than it needs to be. One common question I hear is, "How am I going to find someone if I don't date anyone?" My answer is, "How are you going to find the right person by dating?" Dating has been around for many years and it hasn't proven to be of any value in reducing the number of divorces. Quite the opposite, it has caused an increase in the divorce rate.

Bringing two people together for the purpose of marriage is God's responsibility; the single person's responsibility is to trust God to do that. Meeting that special person is an event only God should arrange. This plan is a relief for some, but disappointing for others who like taste-testing their way to their final selection. They enjoy the sorting process and see nothing wrong with it, while the biblical principle teaches us not to sort through people but to discern who that one person is. The best comment I have ever heard on this issue is, "You're not responsible for finding your mate, just for recognizing who they are."

Just knowing God has a specific person for each of us called to marry isn't enough; we still need to know how that relationship begins. We know that the specific person exists, but where is he or she? Is God hiding that person or are there clues that will be given as to where to look first? How do we locate that person, or do they even need to be located at all?

The Bible says, *"He who finds a wife finds what is good and receives favor from the LORD"* (Prov 18:22). Does the word *find* mean to frantically search or conduct an investigation? No, it is referring to finding along the way. The word *find* as used here is a translation from the Hebrew word matsa' (maw-tsaw'); a primitive root; properly, to **come forth** to, i.e. **appear** or exist; transitively, to attain, i.e. find or acquire; figuratively, to occur, meet or be present. Think of it more as a surprise discovery rather than the results of an effort put into searching.

How Finding Along the Way Works

How does someone meet the person they will eventually marry if they don't search for them? By following God's plan for their life. It doesn't matter if that specific person is on the other side of the world. When both follow God's plan, their paths will eventually bring them together to walk side by side. God brings two people together through parallel paths. It is the blending of two preordained plans. In His plan the paths run parallel right next to each other. This may happen once or several times temporarily, eventually it becomes permanent. He does not have them meet at an intersection where two paths cross once for a brief time, never to cross again.

Some incorrectly worry that they have missed their "intersection moment." This belief comes from a lack of understanding of God's character. In most cases, people feel this way because of something wrong they have done. Because of this wrong they believe God is punishing them by taking away His best plan for their life. This belief is way off track! God's character consists of mercy and grace; His gifts and callings are without repentance.

With parallel paths it is possible that a couple may know each other and be unaware that the other person is their future mate. It is not necessary to have "love at first sight." The joining together of two paths and the revelation of the future bonding isn't always simultaneous. This may be disappointing for those who believe they have to match the Hollywood induced idea of what is romantic. But when two people know each other apart from romantic interest, it allows two things: an honest look at what the other person is really like, no false fronts, and a friendship that is not based on romantic interests.

Finding Along the Way Requires Trust and Contentment

Some have a hard time trusting God when it comes to finding a mate. I've seen many people question the fact that it is God who brings two people together because they couldn't figure out how He could do that? How is He going to bring two people together without either one of them actively looking for the other person? Some allow this to become a stumbling block; if they don't know the exact details before the journey then they are not going to take the trip. Imagine dismissing a biblical truth because of an inability to comprehend how an all-knowing, all-powerful God could do something! This is clearly a lack of faith and understanding of who God is. In Hebrews 10:38, we are told, *"But my righteous one will live by faith. And if he shrinks back, I will not be pleased with him."*

The Bible does not tell us how the mate-discovery plan happens in every case, nor does it have to happen the exact same way for all. We must go on the journey in faith, knowing that's what God wants us to do. He should be allowed to be the one who brings two people together. The real question is, can we trust Him to do that? Where trust doesn't exist, fear always will replace it. If a person cannot trust God in this area, then fear will cause him or her to do something that is out of His will.

This principle of faith is illustrated in Mark, chapter four, in the parable of the growing seed. In verse 26, we are given an illustration of what the kingdom of heaven is like. It is like a man scattering seed on the ground. After he plants it, it doesn't matter if he sleeps or is awake, the seed sprouts and the man doesn't have to even know how it does that. It is not knowing how it will happen that makes it happen; it is just believing that it will.

In God's pattern for marriage, as found in Genesis, chapter two, what did Adam do to find his mate? What was he doing just before he met Eve? He was sleeping—not searching, but sleeping. Sleeping represents trust and peace. Adam didn't have to search for Eve, God brought her to him.

To believe mate discovery is God's responsibility, a person must be content with his/her present circumstances, knowing He has a plan and a purpose for the situation that the person is currently in. Trusting Him with the desire to someday be married can only be accomplished by having and keeping our focus on others as we live a life of service. What makes contentment so important is that it takes a lot of patience to allow God to determine the timing of this event. There is an appointed time for that discovery. It is the best time for getting a relationship started, but it's not necessarily your timing.

So, what should a person be doing while waiting for this to happen? They should be following God's plan for those who are single (as found in 1 Co. 7:32-35), doing selfless acts of service on the Lord's behalf.

Finding a mate is not a reward for following God's plan for singleness, it is a by-product of it. Following biblical principles shouldn't be used as another means to get what you want. You should not judge these principles by how well they serve your agenda. You should not try them out just to see if they work. This is not something a person should try contingent upon gaining desired results within a certain time period. Successful dating does not mean getting married at an early age. I'm not trying to teach you ten steps on how to get your mate. I don't ever want to teach anything that will allow you to act independent of God. Following these biblical principles should be a lifelong commitment, no matter how long the plan takes, or at what age a person is.

Biblical Contradictions with Searching

Searchers, however, are not content in their present circumstances; they are always anxiously looking to change things. They live in a state of constantly being on the edge of a relationship they have always dreamed of. The possibility seems so close, yet reality often proves otherwise. Searchers have been caught up by society into believing there is something they must do to either make someone come to them or to locate where that right person is. This distraction paralyzes that person from being able to give one-hundred percent to God.

Searching isn't biblical because it doesn't match with God's call for being single. It doesn't allow the undivided, undistracted devotion to the Lord required in 1 Corinthians 7:35. A searcher's interest is divided and he/she cannot give one hundred percent to God. The desire to marry is a legitimate one, but wrong focus is a major distraction.

People who are desperate searchers do so because they are trying to fill a need in their life. They don't feel needed or loved, and so are insecure. Their disillusionment with life has caused discontent. Their focus is on themselves and what they don't have, rather on what they could be giving to others. They believe their discontent is the result of not being in a relationship with someone, that all their problems would disappear if they had that relationship. All such problems can be solved through a proper biblical view of life and our personal relationship with God.

Following God's timing isn't an issue to searchers. They initiate the search because they believe they are in control of their destiny. They take it upon themselves to decide when they want to "settle down." Because searchers don't believe that God has a specific person reserved for them, they are under pressure to hurry so someone else doesn't get to the man/woman of their dreams before they do. Evidence of this belief is found in comments like "They married late." Late according to whose standards? Is there a predetermined age that every person should get married? No, God's plan for each individual doesn't have to be the same for each person.

Searching is believed by searchers to be a two-step process. The first part is meeting the person. This by itself is usually not enough; searchers must now go to the next step. They must decide whether or not that person is the one they believe they should enter into a relationship with. They can't tell just by looking.

So, the second step dictates that a romantic relationship has to take place to determine if that person is the one or not. Therefore, these searchers are in and out of multiple relationships searching for the right person. The belief here is that there is nothing wrong with having a relationship for the purpose of confirming if their hunch about this person was correct. The belief that it is acceptable to cross the boundary of a brother/sister relationship for any other reason than for marriage is a lowering of God's standard.

Once society accepted this false notion to lower God's standard in that area then other unbiblical reasons for having a relationship crept in. When opposite sex relationships became temporary it made it difficult for anyone to tell the difference between a relationship that was for the purpose of searching or for physical entertainment only. People were now able to have a relationship strictly to fulfill the lust of the flesh with no intention of marriage under the disguise of searching. Because who could tell the difference from the outside? Perhaps they look the same, but the difference is on the inside and it involves the motive of the heart.

One day, while I was at work, the man I was working with tried to call my attention to a woman who was walking by that he was lusting after. In a kind and non-judgmental way, I declined to participate in his immoral behavior. He was immediately embarrassed and began to make an excuse that it was fine for him to do that because he was single. Whether you are married or single there is no excuse to lust after someone.

Searching is often exciting and stimulating, which makes it addictive. I went to a Promise Keeper's convention once with a man who was a searcher. Since the convention was for men only, this man was in unfamiliar territory. He couldn't spend his time checking out females in the group. There were, however, concession stands that had women working at them. The man's withdrawal symptoms were so great that having spotted those women he made an immediate beeline towards them to strike up a friendly conversation.

Searching has many drawbacks. It's a time-consuming distraction from God's plan for singleness; it causes people to cross the boundary of the brother/sister relationship, and it has an addictive characteristic that carries over into marriage. This is no surprise because it is not God's method of bringing two people together for the purpose of marriage. On the other hand, finding along the way has many benefits. It has the time-redeeming quality that allows someone to fulfill God's plan for their life, it protects the marriage relationship from unfaithfulness both before and after the wedding, and it shows how special a person's marriage partner is. Again this is not shocking because it is God's plan.

CHAPTER 7

GENUINE LOVE

What Love Isn't

Throughout the ages much has been sung, said, and written about what people think love relationships are. Unfortunately, there is a ton of **misinformation** out there. People have given different meanings to what love really is. Subsequently, many wrong acts have been committed in the name of love. It is far too common to pick up a newspaper and read about people who have killed someone they have claimed to "love." I'm not quite sure what the killer's definition could possibly be. But it's a fact that the wrong definition of love in the male and female relationship has been a source of many serious problems throughout history.

The definition of love has been reduced by some to mean only receiving a pleasure, a good feeling, or the approval of one's lifestyle. People use the word to explain an emotion they receive through things that bring them enjoyment. "I love chocolate." "I love skiing." "I love my car." However, love becomes destructive when based **only** on someone else's ability to bring us enjoyment or make us feel good. It is wrong and worldly to think of love toward another person as just another means to get pleasure.

Worldly love is always given in response to the pleasure another person has given to us. It works like this, you give me pleasure, I'll give you pleasure. Love is the reward for pleasure given. No pleasure received means no love will be given. But Jesus asks, *"If you love those who love you, what reward will you get?"* (Matt 5:46-47).

Many also believe that love is always the same as approval—"If I agree with your beliefs and actions then I can love you." They believe they cannot love someone unless they agree 100% with how that person is living. This conditional type of love causes hesitancy in giving love to everybody. Fortunately, God does not love like that. If He did, He could not love any of us.

Using the wrong definition of love doesn't allow someone to remain or increase in love. Today we see many marriages end in divorce simply because one or both of the people no longer "feel in love" with each other. That's not biblical. Ephesians chapter five tells us, "Husbands love your wives." There are no conditions to that or exceptions. It is a decision to love. The world believes love just happens to you; you have no control over it, therefore it is impossible to measure or increase it. In this stupid, cupid-type love, one gets hit by a whim and has nothing to do with love's coming or going! If you have no say in it, then it's impossible to control, to measure and to increase it.

Today, we see people "fall in love" based on how cute someone is. Do you really want someone to love you based on how cute you are? How are they going to love you more? You would have to get cuter, and sorry to say, but you are about as cute as you are ever going to get right now. Therefore, if they love you because you're cute, they will never love you more than they do right now.

Many falsely believe that romantic love is the highest type of love relationship because of its sky-high emotions. This thinking caters to the idea that love is another word for enjoyment. While love may produce intense physical and emotional feelings, it is not the highest form of love. Feelings by themselves are not love.

Feelings or emotions can lie to you, they can't always be trusted. People go to horror movies to enjoy the feeling of being scared. The reality is that while they're emotionally frightened with heart racing and adrenaline rushing, nothing is actually happening to them. It's a good example of how emotions can lie to you and can't always be trusted. You can have a feeling about something and it is not necessarily true. In fact, all movies are really emotional aerobics. And that's why the favorites are usually the "feel good movie of the year." The "I laughed, I cried" shows.

Love is Not Abstract

People do not get to choose the definition of love. Love is not abstract, or subject to whims or opinions. Love is the most defined term there is. It is described in each of the 66 books of the Bible. Love is not an arbitrary term, it's inalienable, which means "not capable of being transferred to a new owner." Therefore, the definition of love cannot be changed by anybody but God. You do not get to choose what love is—it is already predetermined. and defined. *Biblical love means following the biblical guidelines of the type of relationship that God has ordained for you to have with a particular person.* So, to love someone, you have to know what type of relationship God wants you to have with that person as well as the guidelines for that type of relationship.

The supernatural aspect is a necessary part of love. Often it has been minimized to the point that it is overlooked. If love were just finding pleasure in something, then it wouldn't be part of the fruit of the Spirit. See Galatians, 5:22; love is the first thing mentioned in the list given there. Also, 1 John 4:7 tells us "that love comes from God." *"Dear friends, let us love one another for love comes from God. Every one who loves has been born of God."* The proof of love is in the sacrifices made. It is not natural to sacrifice, love drives you to it.

That's certainly a different kind of love. The way Jesus commanded us to love is a noticeably different manner. *"A new commandment I give to you, love one another as I have loved you. By this all men will know that you are my disciples because you love one another"* (John13: 34-35). People should be able to tell when someone is loving someone else as the result of following Jesus.

Currently some Christians are not acting like the disciples of Jesus in the way we love. Particularly, people are not drawn to Jesus by the way the Church presently is conducting their male/female relationships. In many cases we are conducting those relationships the same way the rest of society is. If we are supposed to be noticeably different, **why** would we want to copy the world in this vital area?

When we learn how to biblically love someone, it becomes easy to measure our love and that is important. How will we ever know if we are increasing in love if we can't measure where we have been and where we are now? Shouldn't we all be increasing in love? Let's not blame the world by saying that the divorce epidemic is the result of direct rebellion. In many cases it is merely the result of a lack of knowing how to love. The divorce epidemic exists today partially as a result of Christians not knowing and acting on the biblical instruction as to how to love. The secular world view isn't totally to blame!

Sadly, the majority of the Church isn't currently upholding the one biblical standard of love. If we, the Church, teach love as an emotional, abstract, nebulous term, then we can't hold people accountable to that standard. How can you hold people accountable to a standard that changes according to rising and falling emotions? We have failed to do what Jesus commissioned us to do, which is to make disciples.

Relationships

Love is all about relationships. All true love relationships should function under this biblical definition of that relationship. All relationships conducted outside God's guidelines are not love relationships (see Romans 13:8). True love is relating to someone the way God intends you to relate to them. A relationship is how you relate to and treat someone. If you call someone your brother, you should treat him as a brother. Rather than seeing love as a means of approval, or a pleasure received, see it as a biblical relationship. If you don't, you won't be able to love everybody, only a select few, and them not very well.

The Bible is a book about relationships, in fact that's all it's about. When Jesus was asked what is the greatest commandment in the Bible, He boiled the whole Book down to two relationships, loving God and loving your fellow man (see Matt 22:37-40). The Ten Commandments are just relationship guidelines. The Bible defines every necessary type of social relationship. *"His divine power has provided every thing we need pertaining to life and godliness"* (2 Peter 1:3). So we have all we need to know about the different relationships that are taught as being biblically correct. The Bible's first and primary focus is on the relationship God has to man. Then it describes what man's relationship is to be toward the Father. The Bible also covers relationships between people. It is filled with examples of good relationships as well as bad ones.

God's love for us is His relationship to us. I'm glad the Bible didn't say that God so loved the world that He gave us all a big kiss. Jesus is our savior. Whether we believe and accept Him as our savior or not, doesn't change who He is! He is our Provider, our Strength in time of need, our Healer, our Comforter, and any other attribute the Bible ascribes to Him. None of these things depend on us. His relationship toward us is not based on what we can do for

Him or what we deserve. However, receiving the benefits of God's relationship toward us does require our faith.

Unconditional love means maintaining a love relationship with someone even if that love is not returned. It doesn't mean that you have to find pleasure in that person. For example, my daughters are my daughters whether they are making me happy or not. That is the relationship. I choose to have a relationship with them and that choice shouldn't be dependent upon whether or not they are giving me enjoyment or not.

God's love for us is unconditional because His relationship to us never changes. *"Nothing can separate us from the love of God"* (see Romans 8:38). In other words, nothing can separate us from His relationship to us. Nothing can separate us from the relationship God has with us. His motive is pure. He considers faithfulness to the relationship more important than the benefits that can be received from that relationship. Again this is not a case of loving only those who love you (see Matt 5:46).

Relationships work best when the two people who are relating to each other are together fulfilling each of the guidelines for that one relationship. This is not always the case. Sometimes relating to someone can be one-sided. This is the difference between having a relationship "to," or having a relationship "with" someone. God's love relationship to the world is sometimes one-sided. *"But God demonstrates his own love for us in this: While we were still sinners, Christ died for us"* (Romans 5:8). God has fulfilled his part of the relationship, and is not dependent on us. *"If we are faithless, he will remain faithful, for he cannot disown himself"* (2 Tim 2:13).

Some relationships unite two people under the same set of relationship guidelines, such as brother to brother. Other relationships unite two people under two different sets of relationship guidelines, such as parent to child and child to parent. Ephesians 6:1 says, *"Children, obey your parents in the Lord."* [**Never is it mentioned anywhere in the Bible that parents should obey their children.**]

One of the problems we are having today is that children have been given more power than their role in the family relationship warrants. In some cases, it seems the children are raising the parents and are running the home. That is unbiblical and unhealthy for the relationship and the society.

The Three Elements of Love

All relationships have three elements: origin, type, and guidelines. True love relationships can only exist where the origin, type, and guidelines being used are biblically based. All three of the elements are needed in a successful love relationship.

The first element of any relationship is **origin**. Whose decision created this relationship? Some relationships you have no choice in, such as who your parents and siblings are. However, we can choose most of our relationships. In relationships that you do choose, it is wise to allow God to be the one to make that decision. Psalm 127:1 advises, *"Unless God builds a house a man labors in vain."* I would add to that, why waste your time with something God didn't ordain? When you have the choice, be led by God's Spirit as to which relationship to be in.

The second element of any relationship is **type**. There are several different types of biblical relationships—husband/wife, parent/child, brother/sister, employer/employee, those in authority/those under authority. All these relationships are in the Bible. Just like the definition of love, people do not get to choose what types of relationships there are. There are some perversions of relationships that are just not biblically condoned in the Scriptures. God is the one who chooses what types of relationships He wants us to have with each other. When people walk outside of this, they are in sin. All types of love relationships are equal in value, but may have different priorities.

The third element of any relationship is **guidelines**. Communicated or not, every relationship has them. Some are just assumed or hidden. Examples of someone's personal guidelines that aren't always spelled out might be: "This relationship will last as long as you bring excitement to me" and "This relationship will last until I find someone else who will bring **more** excitement to me." Hidden guidelines are enforced as though they were communicated. Love belongs to God. The guidelines He expects us to follow are communicated to us throughout the Bible.

Each type of biblical relationship has its own distinct guidelines which are unique to each of the different types of relationships. Because there are different guidelines, it becomes vitally important to first define the type of relationship. The guidelines for each type of relationship are in addition to the minimum that are common to all types of love relationships.

The minimum set of guidelines for any relationship is that extended to our fellowman, or what the Bible refers to as a neighbor. I looked up all the "one another" verses in the Bible; that list is the minimum we are to be doing. Jesus said, *"You have heard that it was said, 'Love your neighbor and hate your enemy.' But I tell you: Love your enemies and pray for those who persecute you"* (Matt 5:43-44). With those words God raised the standard of how we should relate to one another under the New Testament. Thus, the minimum set of guidelines for any person regardless of your relationship to them would be as a neighbor. Every relationship starts with that minimum set of guidelines, and in most cases others added along to them.

If you have an employer, the minimum set of guidelines to be used in that relationship would be as a fellowman or a neighbor **plus** the guidelines that are specifically for an employer (see Col 3:22-24). If your employer is a believer then there are additional guidelines to follow. *"Those who have believing masters are not to show less respect for them because they are brothers. Instead, they are to* *serve them even better, because those who benefit from their service are believers, and dear to them. These are the things you are to teach and urge on them"* (1 Tim 6:2). In this situation you have to follow the guidelines of a fellow man, an employer and a believing employer. [It's amazing how some Christians want to take advantage of their Christian employer, yet that is opposite of what the Bible says.]

The more guidelines you follow, the more you love. This makes love measurable. It's not an ooey, gooey feeling that cannot be explained or measured. *"This is how we know [yes, we can know] that we love the children of God: by loving God and carrying out his commands. This is love for God: to **obey his commands**. And his commands are not burdensome"* (1 John 5:2-3). The commands mentioned here are the same as guidelines; both mean the same thing. When one or the other of my daughters doesn't want to obey, I ask her, "Do you love me?" "Yes, Daddy, I love you," she responds. "But if you love me, you will obey me." This puts this concept in a concrete form that my children can understand.

People are now referring to certain crimes as hate crimes. Biblically speaking all crimes are hate crimes. Is there such a thing as a love crime? No, all crimes are in violation of the guidelines of a relationship resulting from not loving that person (see Romans 13:8-10).

What is love in one type of relationship may not be love in another type. We wouldn't need different types of relationships if the guidelines were all the same. But because of the difference in guidelines, love depends upon knowing what type of relationship we are in. Am I going to love you as, a brother, a spouse, etc. For example, as a married man, can I love another woman? Yes, I can. In fact, **I must**. God has commanded us to love one another. The qualifier of that question is that I must live within the guidelines of a sister relationship. It would be sin to love outside the boundaries set by the guidelines that are specifically for a spouse.

When, as a married man, I asked, "Can I love another woman?" the natural tendency was for the hearer to think of love in terms of romance. Of course, as we discussed previously, the only biblical relationship that has romance in its guidelines is the husband/wife relationship, never a brother/sister relationship or those not intended to result in marriage. This viewpoint is contrary to the culturally defined practice of dating. Nevertheless, it is the truth.

Using sex in the wrong type of relationship is sexual immorality. The biblical definition of sexual immorality is the use of any of our sexual functions with someone other than a marriage partner, for the purpose of sexual stimulation, either thought, sight, touch, or intercourse. It would be wrong to say that any form of sex in any other relationship outside of marriage (union between a man and a woman) would be love. Romans 13:8-9 tells us that it is unloving to be sexually immoral. However, many people today consider sex outside of marriage as a loving act.

A woman called into a radio program and said she had a hard time staying away from sex outside of marriage because she was a loving person. What a self-serving rationalization! Contrary to public opinion, sex outside of marriage is not love. There is no such thing as "making love" outside of marriage. Only in the context of marriage is the sexual act love. Again, the culturally defined dating practice commonly violates this truth. Not only does it violate it, but sexual immorality is often the central focus.

When a man looks upon a woman other than a spouse for the purposes of sexual stimulation, he is traveling outside the guidelines of a brother/sister type relationship and is therefore sinning. What Jesus wants us to do is not use any of our sexual functions including thought, sights, or touch for the purposes of sexual stimulation unless we are in a marriage relationship. Jesus said *"You have heard that it was said, 'Do not commit adultery.' But I tell you that anyone who looks at a woman lustfully has already committed adultery with her in his heart"* (Matt 5:27-28).

So, what does it mean to say "I love you"? It should mean that you are going to have the type of relationship God wants you to have with that particular person. You are informing someone that your intentions are to have a biblical relationship with them and to follow God's guidelines for that relationship. Don't look at love as a means of approval, or pleasure received. True love is relating to someone the way God wants you to. True love is following the biblical guidelines of the type of relationship that God has ordained for you to have with a particular person. To go outside of these boundaries set by biblical guidelines is disobedience to the Father who loves us unconditionally and eternally.

CHAPTER 8

THE DATING NAME GAME

Different Types of Relationships

Much is being said in Christian circles today about opposite-sex relationships. Books, newsletter articles, and radio programs are discussing this subject, with those discussions centered on the different types of relationships that are entered into during singleness. A confusing array of names, such as dating, courtship, betrothal, Christian dating and recreational dating have been attached to these relationships. There is even a book written on "dateship," that combines dating with courtship.

In a recent radio interview, an author of a book about dating versus courtship claimed that dating was "better" than courtship. To understand his argument, I tried to find clues as to which definition of dating he was using. I was curious as to how he could make such a claim, and why he would. Given the problems we have with divorce in this country, I couldn't understand why anyone would want to defend dating.

Over the many years of ministry to single adults, I've seen clearly that using the word *dating* actually is confusing. Dating is a catch-all word used to describe all sorts of relationships. When I mentioned the word to a group of people, I found out that what I was refer-ring to and what they were thinking of was often different. There were probably as many different definitions as there were people in the group. Therefore, it makes the subject difficult to discuss. *Dating* has many distinct definitions while *courtship* applies only to relationships that are intended to lead to marriage.

What makes it more confusing is people claim their relation-ship is under one heading when they are actually following an-other. Some couples say they are courting when they are actually dating. Christian dating, for the most part, is worldly dating but to a different degree. Christian dating is sometimes just sinning "responsibly." Some claim their relationship is Christian because of who their relationship is with, because both are Christians. But who the relationship is with doesn't make the relationship Chris-tian. How the relationship is conducted and the guidelines that are followed does.

The reason for the confusion is that there isn't an authoritative or universal definition for these two terms. It's interesting to note that neither *dating* nor *courtship* is used in the Bible. And, there isn't a complete explanation in the dictionary for either word. So, without an official definition for these two terms, who could say which of the different definitions is right or wrong? Although the words are not used in the Bible, the relationship they are sometimes trying to describe is. So, don't get trapped in the dating name game; don't be hung-up on names that have no absolute meaning.

We can eliminate the confusion if we just explain that we are trying to describe the relationships used with the opposite-sex during singleness. Opposite-sex relationships during singleness are definitely described in the Bible, both in chapter and verse, and in biblical principles. ***Biblically only two, very separate, types of opposite-sex relationships are to be entered into in singleness: The brother-sister relationship and the pre-marriage relationship.*** We can avoid confusion by recognizing just these two types. Although it's easier to say "dating" than "biblical opposite-sex relationships used during singleness," we must be careful not to sacrifice clarity for brevity. We must be able to accurately examine opposite-sex relationships, and be able to discern which are and which are not biblical in beliefs and behaviors.

Brother/Sister Relationships

The first biblical opposite-sex relationship for those who are single is the brother/sister relationship. How should someone treat his or her **spiritual** brothers or sisters? First Timothy 5:1-2 tells us that all members of the opposite-sex should be treated the same way as someone would treat a natural brother or sister. First Timothy 5:1-2 in the Phillips translation tells us; "Treat younger women as sisters, and no more. "There should be concern for their well-being, and a desire to see spiritual growth in their lives. Also, since you care about their physical and spiritual well-being, you should avoid situations and actions that may cause them to stumble.

You would never consider a romantic relationship with a sibling or use him or her as a means to receive sexual stimulation of any kind. Natural brothers or sisters are **never** thought of as potential mates. Therefore there is no reason to "check" them out. Of course, that's not what you will hear on TV or read in a magazine, for that is contrary to our society's present standards. According to those standards it is expected that people use everybody of the opposite sex as fair game for sexual stimulation.

A Boundary for Sexual Stimulation

God, on the other hand, has set an emotional and a physical boundary for sexual stimulation between brothers and sisters. First Thessalonians 4:6 KJV says, in reference to sexual immorality, *"That no man go beyond and defraud his brother in any matter."* The word *brother* is not referring to just males, it is referring to our fellowman; so, this verse applies to both men and women. The phrase "go beyond" refers to overstepping a boundary.

Since, biblically, the marriage relationship is the only relationship where sexual stimulation is permissible, genetic as well as fraternal brother/sister relationships that are used for the purpose of sexual stimulation are sexually immoral. Therefore, physical and emotional abstinence is part of the brother/sister relationship. That message again won't make it onto a television news special nor appear on a magazine cover, but emotional abstinence is just as much a part of the brother/sister relationship as physical abstinence is. Although crossing the emotional boundary may not be as obvious as the physical; nevertheless, emotional abstinence is still a requirement for sexual purity.

These boundaries will be crossed when a person does not believe that God is the one who decides which two people will marry each other. Believing God has a specific person chosen for that person to marry makes it easy to desire that relationship and want to wait and forego involving themselves in counterfeit relationships.

What about "friendships" with the opposite sex? Does God condone such relationships? Certainly—if the friendship is truly that. Unfortunately, some people claim to be just friends with a person of the opposite-sex, but that "friendship" is for the purpose of checking the other person out. This is a violation of the biblical standard for brother/sister relationships. It is really dating with the tag of friendship. Sometimes people hide behind the word "friends" to do wrong.

Using friendship to check someone out is not a true friendship because the relationship will end once the decision is made that this person is not "the one." On the other hand, friendship in a true brother/sister relationship never has to end. Real friendship is not withdrawn because a person doesn't get what he/she wants. Would someone make a friend with their natural brother or sister just to check them out? That type of relationship lies between the brother/sister and pre-marriage relationships. Since it is in-between the two, that makes it neither one nor the other and so it becomes unbiblical.

It is a very different relationship when you say someone is your girlfriend than when you say a girl is your friend. Many times one person in an ongoing relationship will say he/she wants to be "just friends." What they are implying is that they have crossed over into a relationship that is intended to go to marriage, but now they want to go back to a brother/sister relationship.

Unbiblical opposite-sex relationships cause divisions within youth groups, singles groups and Churches. People whom God never intended to be involved in a romantic relationship break up. Then what happens? They don't want to see each other, so they leave the Church to avoid seeing the other person. Friends in the group begin taking sides and create divisions. This is just not what God intended the Church to be about.

Defrauding

Going past the boundaries of a brother/sister relationship and doing something that belongs only in a marital relationship defrauds. First Thessalonians 4:6 in the Phillips translation says, *"If you step over the boundary you will steal, cheat and exploit your fellowman."* The purpose of this particular defrauding is to gain sexual stimulation from another person, thus stealing pleasures from them. The only person you should receive sexual stimulation from is your spouse. In consensual sexual stimulation before marriage, what is often being stolen are the emotions and affections that belong to someone else—a future spouse! Defrauding is stealing the innocence of another person.

Defrauding is a word with an interesting connotation. The word *defraud* means to cheat out of, scam, deceive, use trickery, swindle, dupe, pose as an impostor, or to misrepresent. It is different than stealing from someone without their knowledge, such as a thief in the night. There is stealing with out someone's knowledge and defrauding which is stealing with trickery. To defraud someone implies that the deceiver has gained consent, there must be a willing party. Back in the '60s a popular concept was born that said it was OK to have sex outside of marriage as long as it was between two consulting adults. That definitely is not a biblical concept. Just because someone **allows** someone else to steal from them does not make the theft right.

Defrauding deceives someone into thinking that one thing is going on when something else really is. To defraud in a relationship means to send the message that you are committed for life in order to win someone's heart only to later back out of that commitment. It is thievery to influence others to win or gain someone's romantic affections while knowing that there is even the slightest possibility that you would back out of the relationship. Allowing another person's romantic affections to be given to you should only be acceptable when you know there will be a lifetime marriage covenant between the two parties. I saw an ad on a bulletin board that read: "Wedding dress for sale—never used," I couldn't help but think that although the dress was never used, the affections of the bride-to-be were. A relationship someone had promised would last forever was now over. All of the expectations of the promise of being married were now gone. This bride-to-be was defrauded.

Pre-marital relationships that are not followed through deceive the participants by claiming with their actions, "This is OK. You don't have to save all your emotions and affections for the person you will someday marry; give some of them to me." Acting on that false premise means you are cheating a future spouse out of the blessings you can bestow by saving all of your emotions and all of your affections for him/her. That is a tragic violation of an awesome gift! No person should want to have these gifts stolen from them nor should they be willing to steal them from someone else. Stealing from one's spiritual brother or sister is even worse.

The deception in this scenario is that sexual immorality, or lust, is being disguised as love. Some call their immorality love, and biblically that is just not true. Once someone crosses over the boundaries of a brother/sister relationship with someone they will never marry they have defrauded them and committed an adulterous act. Adultery is the exact opposite of love; it is sin. True love follows the commandments, and that decision keeps us from harming our fellowman. Romans 13:9-10 *"Love does no harm to its neighbor. Therefore love is the fulfillment of the law." Do not commit adultery," "Do not murder," "Do not steal," "Do not covet," and whatever other commandment there may be, are **summed up** in this one rule: "Love your neighbor as yourself."*

To love someone you have to fulfill the commandments! Is it loving to steal from somebody? No! Is it loving to murder someone? No! Is it loving to covet other people's mates and possessions? No! So if these three commandments are not loving, then how can anyone say it is loving to commit adultery when it is the first sin listed out of the four in verse nine. If you break even one of the commandments you are doing something that is not love. It is not up to us to decide which of the commandments can be violated and still be love. Therefore, any relationship that crosses over the boundaries of a brother/sister relationship with someone that is not the specific person God intends for them to marry is not love.

God Wants Strong and Pure Marriages

Sexual immorality prior to or after a wedding weakens the institution of marriage. Physical and emotional sexual immorality **is** adultery. One way to grasp the concept is to consider the word *adulterated*. Webster's definition is, "To make **inferior** by adding a harmful, inferior or unnecessary substance." If my car were running out of gas and there was no gas station close-by, could I just pour water into the tank and hope I made it to the next safe spot? Of course not! I would go nowhere because my gas would have been adulterated: the added substance was harmful and inferior. So adulterated relationships are inferior because once the boundary has been crossed a harmful and unnecessary substance has been added. A strong marriage is an unadulterated one.

Crossing over the emotional and physical boundaries damages relationships. When someone does something that belongs only in a marital relationship with someone who is never going to be their spouse they have committed adultery against their own future spouse, their partner in that act, and that partner's future spouse. We are warned not to do this when we are told in Exodus 20:17, *"You should not covet your neighbor's wife."* This commandment should be applied throughout a person's whole life, not merely after the wedding. We must use the principle if you shouldn't be doing something after you get married you shouldn't be doing it before. If you are expected to not be kissing anyone but your spouse after you are married, then don't kiss other people before you are married.

One danger of going past sexual boundaries is the creation of memories with someone who is never going to be your spouse. Marriage is an exclusive relationship and memories created with someone other than your spouse take away from that exclusiveness. Even if the people those memories are created with are completely out of your life, the memories continue.

[3] What would a young bride think about all the groom's old girlfriends standing alongside her at the marriage altar? How about being with them on their wedding night? Just because previous partners are not physically present doesn't mean they are not there in thought. Yes, forgiveness is available, but it doesn't exempt us

---

[3] Joshua Harris I Kissed Dating Goodbye

from ever thinking about prior experiences again. But those who still are pure, especially our children, can enter this marital relationship without harmful memories. All their "firsts" can go to one person! What a blessing that will be to all involved.

People who use a legalistic view of the "do not covet your neighbor's wife" commandment may say, "If someone is not married, it's OK to covet after them." Unfortunately, legalistic viewpoints of the law only concern themselves with the technicality of the rule, while the spirit of the law concerns itself with the reason the law was written in the first place.

So, what was God's purpose in this law? He was trying to protect the sanctity of marriage. Applying this law both before and after someone is married does just that. This principle is exactly what Jesus described in Matthew, chapter five, when He spoke about murder, adultery, divorce, oaths, an eye for an eye and love for your enemy.

Before we go on, let's make it perfectly clear that I am not saying that knowing whom you are going to marry gives you the freedom to be sexually involved with them. People still need to be physically abstinent until marriage vows are taken. It is still damaging to use any sexual function prior to marriage even with the person they will eventually marry.

It is necessary to have a complete and total separation between all brother/sister relationships and the specific person God has chosen to be your mate to have a pure marriage. This is the only way to avoid the damage done by crossing the boundaries of a brother/sister relationship. In-between relationships are unbiblical. Either you are in a brother/sister relationship with someone or you are not.

Allowing God to be the one who brings two people together keeps the separation between the two types of relationships. If there is to be any change in relationships, it should begin with God's revelation of who the specific person is. This will prevent entering into any pre-marriage relationship not ordained by Him. Going from a brother/sister relationship to a pre-marriage relationship with someone can happen in a moment, in a twinkling of an eye. The revelation of whom your mate is brings immediate change to your life. That is why people must be prepared for the responsibility of marriage prior to God's revelation

If you are already guilty of this sin cut your losses immediately and don't cause any more damage. I'm not saying that people can't be forgiven, just that this situation should be avoided. As with Abraham and Ishmael, forgiveness doesn't mean there won't be consequences brought about by a wrongful act.

I'm not condemning anyone who has experienced the world's negative dating patterns. Memories created outside of a husband/wife relationship can cause problems within a marriage, but you're not doomed if this has happened to you. It doesn't do any good to feel bad about the past because you can't change it. What you can do is change your belief about it so it doesn't cause any more harm in the future to you or anybody else.

Pre-Marriage Relationships

We have discussed the biblical brother/sister relationship. Now let's consider the second biblical opposite-sex relationship for single adults—I call it the pre-marriage relationship. The pre-marriage relationship is one that is entered into for the purpose of marriage preparation. It's not a trial to see if a marriage will work. The truth is that it's impossible to practice marriage! Society promotes the idea that all we have to do is live together before marriage in a trial period and we could reduce the divorce rate. In real life, this concept has increased the divorce rate to [4] 80% in those who lived together first over those who did not. You cannot try marriage. Doing the things of marriage is not marriage. You are either

[4] National Bureau of Economic Research

married to someone or you are not. **Marriage requires a *lifetime* commitment to one person**.

The pre-marriage relationship has similarities to the brother/sister relationship. Physical abstinence is still practiced. That makes it special when the groom hears, "You may **now** kiss your bride" and the words really mean what they say. Lusting after physical pleasures is still not allowed. Physical intimacy is strictly reserved for after the wedding. But there is a change in the amount of time and attention given to a future spouse during this period. Now that the persons involved have become the number two priority in each other's life (God is #1, of course), it's OK for them to give a large amount of time and attention to each other. Such non-sexual physical and emotional bonding should take place prior to the wedding. It establishes the exclusiveness of the relationship that's going toward marriage.

A good example of the seriousness of this type of relationship is the story of Mary and Joseph. They were engaged to be married when Mary became pregnant. The Bible tells us Joseph thought about divorcing Mary, thinking she had been unfaithful. They weren't married, they were betrothed, similar to what we call engaged, yet the Bible says that Joseph thought about *divorcing* Mary. Betrothal in those days was that binding. Engagement meant something back then. Unlike today, engagement was a serious commitment between a man and a woman, not a trial relationship.

So what should be accomplished during the pre-marriage relationship? The purpose of a pre-marriage relationship is to learn to relate specifically to that particular person. Each person is unique and we relate differently with different people. Two people should know each other well enough that there won't be any big surprises after the wedding. The goal is to blend two unique individuals into one harmonious unit. My personal opinion on engagement is that it should occur after all the relationship issues are worked out and the couple is ready to be married. Then the engagement period should be spent on wedding preparations, not relationship issues.

The pre-marriage relationship takes the pressure off both parties. Their time together is not an interview; there is no need to be phony or to hide anything. Dr. Ken Stewart describes current dating practices as the "art of mutual deception" —two people putting on a front, each trying to impress the other person. People begin relationships based on first impersonation, not first impression. Neither person gives a truthful representation. This is not the case in the pre-marriage relationship. That couple can be totally open and honest. At this point, it is necessary to work on issues that may be obstacles to a marriage. What is it going to take to live like Amos 3:3, *"How can two walk together unless they are agreed?"* This is the time to learn how to walk in agreement. This is where there is a blending of God's pre-ordained plans.

A common misconception is that people who have had a previous marriage really don't need a lot of counseling. They have had "on-the-job training." But this concept also has been proven wrong as can be seen by the high number of second marriages that also end in divorce. Obviously, it doesn't matter how many relationships you have had. You can't practice relating to a specific person by relating to others. After I taught a lesson titled "Methods of Choosing a Mate", one man told me he understood what I was saying but still wanted to date to practice for marriage. Obviously he didn't understand what I was saying. He went on to explain that he needed to date, so he could practice opening doors. You don't need to date to practice opening doors! That was an excuse.

Dealing with Issues

Discovering existing issues is not the determining factor upon which to end a relationship. But, in our society today, some people look at relationships as a way of trying people out. The belief is: Dating is the time to see if you want to be engaged to someone, engagement the time to see if you want to marry that person. These worldly relationships are used for the purpose of trying to figure out if the couple is making a mistake or not. The relationship is one long interview, not decided until the very end. Some people when they get engaged are still involved in negotiations, what they can do to close the deal. Even up to the wedding day they aren't really sure if what they are doing is right.

Under God's plan, each person knows that the other is "the one" before the relationship even starts. If they find there are issues to deal with, that's fine. This is the time to find out. The discovery is a good thing and it doesn't mean the relationship has to end. If you know the person is the one God has chosen for you, you both will work through any issues that arise. That sounds like a good marriage to me! Stay away from the belief that people must be issue-free in order to have them qualify as a marriage partner. That is an interview dating concept and it doesn't work.

To sum up: The two types of biblical opposite-sex relationships that are to be used during singleness are the brother/sister relationship and the pre-marital relationship. It is necessary to have a complete and total separation between all brother/sister relationships and the specific person God has chosen to be your mate. In-between relationships are unbiblical.

These two relationships can be summed-up by answering three questions: How should someone treat a brother or sister? How does someone keep the two separate? What is the purpose of the pre-marriage relationship?

Be careful when you use the words *dating* or *courtship* when you are really talking about are the opposite-sex relationships used during singleness, and the principles behind them. Don't get confused by being caught up in the dating name game!

CHAPTER 9

HOW FAR CAN I GO?

Standards for Sexual Behavior

There are many different standards being used when people define sexual morality; most are well below that described in the Bible. Many Christians today are committing sexual immorality and they don't even know it. They are merely *assuming* the standard they are following is biblical.

The current misunderstandings about sexual morality have helped to fuel the divorce epidemic in our country. This epidemic must be stopped, and Christians must lead the attack. Even though improper actions may be taken in ignorance of God's standard, they still produce negative consequences. The families and children who are harmed by the actions of those who accept immoral standards of sexual behavior cannot differentiate between ignorance and evil. The resulting broken hearts caused by sexual immorality hurt just as much as those caused by defiant wrongdoing. Whether you bump a beehive on purpose or by accident the results are still the same, although, on one hand, ignorance is easier to correct than rebellion to the truth because there is no damage done to your conscience.

To discuss sexual morality we must first define the term. *Morality* can be defined as a standard of what is right and appropriate behavior. Thus, *immorality* defines the state one achieves by not conforming to the principles of right behavior which have been established in that morality. When people are using more than one standard to discuss a topic, more information is needed. So, because there are many standards, if we are to talk about sexual morality we must first define whose standard we are referring to. As committed Christians we should not base our actions on our own or society's standards; we should be led by God's standard.

God's way is not merely a higher standard, it's a different one. It is completely separate from the world's way. Isaiah 55:8-9 God points out here the enormous contrast between His standards and the world's. *"For my thoughts are not your thoughts, neither are your ways my ways," declares the LORD." As the heavens are higher than the earth, so are my ways higher than your ways and my thoughts than your thoughts."* We hear a lot about alternative choices today. The premise is that all choices are acceptable; there are no absolutes.

But God's way is not an alternative to the world's way. It is not merely an improvement of the old or an alternative choice for modern man. 2 Corinthians 5:17 *"If anyone is in Christ, he is a new creation; the old has gone, the new has come."* Therefore, His way and the world's way cannot co-exist; one displaces the other (see James 3:11). Just as darkness is the absence of light and light is absent of darkness so is the world's way the absence of God's way and God's way is absent of the world's. Too often Christians copy the world's system and then try to "Christianize" it. They take a worldly standard and attempt to clean it up, but it still ends up being a worldly standard.

There are no high and low standards in God's will. However there are high and low standards when you compare human efforts to God's will and expectations. A low human standard is one that contains very little or none of God's truth. A high human standard is one that contains mostly God's truth with a little bit of human standard added to it. While it is a high worldly standard is just that—a worldly standard.

That is why the road that leads to destruction is described by Jesus as a wide road; it encompasses high, medium, and low worldly standards. *"Enter through the narrow gate. For wide is the gate and broad is the road that leads to destruction, and many enter through it. But small is the gate and narrow the road that leads to life, and only a few find it,"* Matthew 7:13-14 advises. The narrow path is narrow because there is only one standard in the will of God.

Biblical sexual morality is a narrow and concrete term that is used to describe any sexual function used only within marriage and in a loving manner. For Christians, the biblical standard of sexual morality shouldn't be an option; we should not be asking if would you like your Christianity with or without sexual morality.

Using Sex

Sex itself is not bad. Sex that is being used as an expression of love in the marriage relationship is the correct use of sex. Is pure water, nothing but H_2O with no impurities in it, bad? Of course not; it's a healthy drink. But if you fill your lungs with water, no matter how pure it is, it will kill you. It won't kill you because it's dirty; it will kill you because it is being used in a manner for which it hadn't been intended. So, too with sex. Sex is not bad, nor is it dirty. After all, God created it. However, its purity can only be experienced when it is being used as an expression of love in the marriage relationship.

In today's society we have limited the meaning of the term "having sex" to include only sexual intercourse. Sadly, a lot of Christians today believe that the only way to cross the boundary is by having sexual intercourse. That is certainly one way, but there are many others. The physical use of sex includes any touch that causes sexual stimulation regardless of where that touch takes place on the body. Anything that causes sexual stimulation outside of marriage, whether done by thought or touch—staring at someone, holding hands, kissing—crosses over the boundary. Of course I'm not talking about a kiss like the one you might give to your grandmother. I'm talking about the kiss of passion that creates sexual stimulation. Whether sex is or is not consummated, it is still sex. Don't use the area of touch as a loophole to do what is wrong. Therefore, *sexual immorality* can not be used as a substitute phrase for *immoral sexual intercourse*. Therefore, technically speaking, when you say someone is "having sex" that doesn't necessarily mean sexual intercourse.

The key to judging if something is sexual, is not merely by the action taken, but also by what kind of response is being produced. If touching someone's nose causes sexual stimulation, you are using sex. Even your body is smart enough to know when you're having sex; it releases hormones into the bloodstream when sexually stimulated.

Sex can also be emotional without any physical contact. How do we know that sex is not just a physical act? Jesus told us, *"You have heard that it was said, 'Do not commit adultery.' But I tell you that anyone who looks at a woman lustfully has already committed adultery with her in his heart"* (Matt. 5:27-28). What Jesus was saying is that adultery is more than just the physical act, it also includes thoughts. Nothing physical happened and yet Jesus called it adultery. Thoughts driven by our emotions really do matter and must be kept in check. God never intended for emotions to be used in a romantic or marital way outside of marriage. Therefore, emotional abstinence is just as important to relationships before marriage as physical abstinence is.

The majority of Churches today do not condone the unbiblical use of our sexual functions when it comes to intercourse or certain places of touch. But flirting is often thought of as harmless fun and allowable among singles. I disagree. Flirting is an act that stimulates sexually through sight, speech, and thought. Therefore, it is wrong. We have giggled and winked at this immoral practice for too long. It is against God's standard.

If we merely set up boundaries against physical acts and not against emotional involvement, once the emotional boundaries are crossed, the physical boundaries will eventually follow. It is unwise to think that we could use any part of our being in a way that is intended for marriage without producing a response that is also only intended for marriage. Your body has no idea whether you're married or not. God didn't create different bodies, one for singles and one for married folks. If someone gives their body sexual input, emotional or physical, they should expect that it will want to respond to that input! God made our bodies to respond that way. So, you can't sit through a sexual, adulterous movie and claim it has had no effect on you. That is just not true. The effect may not be immediate or even recognizable, but there will always be an effect.

Human sexual responses are strong and quick to arise when our emotions are triggered. Therefore, it is destructive to use sex as a toy to be played with. If your response to seeing sexual immorality is "it's no big deal it doesn't affect me" then it has already had an effect on you. You have become desensitized to sin and are ready for the next step deeper into it. Therefore, we must conclude, sexual immorality can be defined as any use of sexual functions outside of marriage for the purpose of sexual stimulation, either by thought, sight, touch, or intercourse.

How much deviation from the standard is acceptable to God? First Thessalonians 4:3 in the Phillips translation says, *"God's plan is to make you holy, and that means a **clean cut** with sexual immorality."* We are further warned in Ephesians 5:3: *"But among you there must not be even a **hint** of sexual immorality, or of any kind of impurity, or of greed, because these are improper for God's holy people."* Colossians 3:5 tells us to *"**Put to death**, [KJV says to mortify, which means to starve] therefore, whatever belongs to your earthly nature: sexual immorality, impurity, lust, evil desires and greed, which is idolatry."* How far can you go? How much sexual stimulation is acceptable prior to marriage? It is incorrect to approach sexual immorality from the viewpoint of how far can I go. We are supposed to avoid it, and not have even a hint of sexual immorality. It is not OK even in just small doses. Scripturally speaking, there is absolutely no room for any deviation at all!

However, one of the most frequently asked questions asked by those who are single is, "How far can I go on a date?" My response: "It depends on whether you're walking or driving!" A silly answer to a silly question. The problem with this question is usually the motivation behind it. The motivation for the question often comes from wanting to know how close someone can get to the line and not sin.

What is typically being asked here is, "How close to the line can I get and not make God really mad?" If this is your motivation for the question how far can you go, then you have already gone too far. For a Christian, the question should not be how close can I get to the line, but how can I avoid being even close to the line. The real motive should be, "What can I do to please God?" as instructed in Ephesians 5:10, and to not cause others to stumble. The correct question to be asked here is, "What is sex and how should it be used?" If this two-part question is answered the question of how far can you go becomes irrelevant.

Why Boundaries

Let's talk about why God set up boundaries in the first place. The reason He has provided standards of sexual morality is that they provide protection and security. His standard honors marriage and makes sex special. It protects families and keeps us from making poor choices that take us away from God's plan for our life. God didn't arbitrarily pick sex outside of marriage and decide to make it wrong to take our fun away or as a test. He does not test us with evil. *"When tempted, no one should say, 'God is tempting me.' For God cannot be tempted by evil, nor does he tempt anyone"* (James 1:13). God gives us boundaries for our own good and the good of others. It is either foolish or selfish to cross over them.

Consequences to Sexual Immorality

Sexual immorality is destructive behavior. It is guaranteed to consume your life. It is progressive in nature. A little leads to more, until eventually it can become so frequent in thought that it dominates a person's thinking and choices. Sexual immorality starts as a servant promising pleasure, but eventually it becomes the master. First Corinthians 6:18 tells us that we should *"Flee from sexual immorality. All other sins a man commits are outside his body, but he who sins sexually sins against his own body."*

Sexual immorality is doubly deceptive. Not only is there pleasure through the sexual stimulation, but also there's the added excitement of it being wrong. The Bible tells us that stolen bread tastes sweet. The deceptive thing about sin is that the sweetness doesn't last. *"Bread gained by deceit is sweet to a man, but afterward his mouth will be filled with **gravel**"* (Prov 20:17 NKJ).

Sexually transmitted diseases are a real consequence to sexually immoral behavior. No one has ever died from not having sex, but many have died from being sexually immoral. Knowing the truth about STDs should be a good deterrent against immoral behavior. It is not a perfect deterrent, though, because it doesn't deal with the root problem behind that act—sin. *"The acts of the sinful nature are obvious: sexual immorality, impurity and debauchery"* (Galatians 5:19 NIV). To Christians, the threat of a disease should be the least reason for us to be sexually moral. That threat should be used as an appeal to those who don't care about their relationship with God and other people.

Beliefs about Consequences

Of course, there are always some who know what is sexually moral but choose to do the opposite. They believe they will somehow escape those consequences. Many feel they are in control and what they are doing won't hurt them. They'll be the "lucky" ones! *"Do not be deceived: God cannot be mocked. A man reaps what he sows"* (Gal 6:7). *"Can a man scoop fire into his lap without his clothes being burned? Can a man walk on hot coals without his feet being scorched? So is he who sleeps with another man's wife; **no one who touches her will go unpunished**"* (Prov 6:27-29). Adam and Eve were warned of the consequences of their sin. They chose to ignore it thinking they wouldn't reap those consequences; but they did. And so do we! Some are even willing to accept the consequences by deceiving themselves into thinking the momentary pleasure received is worth the risk.

Looking Down the Road

One of the best advantages a person can have in life is to gain the right perspective. Perspective gives us the ability to look ahead to see where a road is leading, before we travel down it. The advantage gained before a person smokes one cigarette, or experiments with drugs or alcohol can prevent a future trip to the cancer ward or a drug and alcohol rehabilitation center. So, let's look at sexual immorality from the right perspective to find out where that road is leading.

The Bible gives us the advantage of having God's perspective on life. A good example of this is found in Proverbs, chapter five. The chapter is a perspective look at adultery. It is an admonition by a father to his son. It warns him not to get involved with an adulteress. Not only does it tell the son not to, it also tells him what will happen if he does. *"At the **end of your life** you will groan, when your flesh and body are **spent***. *You will say, "How I hated discipline. How my heart spurned correction. I would not obey my teachers or listen to my instructors. I have come to **the brink of utter ruin**_in the midst of the whole assembly."* (Prov 5:11-13) Proverbs 7:25-27 adds, *"Do not let your heart turn to her ways or stray into her paths. Many are the victims she has brought down; her slain are a mighty throng. Her house is a highway to the grave, **leading down to the chambers of death.**"*

Avoiding Sexual Immorality

Some believe that sexual immorality is unavoidable. That is not true! The Bible says, *"So I say, **live by the Spirit, and you will not gratify the desires of the sinful nature"*** (Gal 5:16). That is not only a promise, it's also a powerful instruction. By living in the Spirit the desire to be sexually immoral won't be fulfilled. On the other-hand, if a person doesn't live by the Spirit then it is impossible to not fulfill the lust of the flesh. The grace of God will give us power to overcome our worldly passions and do what is right. *"For the grace of God that brings salvation has appeared to all men.* [12] *It teaches us to say "No" to ungodliness and **worldly passions**, and to live self-controlled, upright and godly lives in this **present age**."* (Titus 2:11-12)

But you can't expect people to abstain from sexual immorality without explaining how to avoid it. How it is done requires God's grace. Simply telling someone not to do something because it's wrong is insufficient. The Bible tells us that those who are prey to sexual immorality lack judgment, there is something missing (see Proverbs 9:4 & 16). Christians must know how to avoid sexual immorality; the Bible teaches us how to have that good judgment.

First Thessalonians 4:3-6 says, *"It is God's will that you should be sanctified: that you should avoid sexual immorality."* We could stop our discussion right here if it were true that we could "just tell someone not to have sex before marriage." If that admonishment were sufficient, there would be no reason for further information. But it goes on to say; [4] *that each one of you <u>know how</u> [or learn] to take a wife for himself in holiness and honor,* [5] *not in the passion of lust like heathen who do not know God;* (RSV) [6] *That no man go beyond and defraud his brother in any matter:* (KJV)

This passage also tells us two ways to avoid sexual immorality. The first point mentioned regarding how to avoid sexual immorality is the correct way to choose a wife: *"That each one of you know how to take a wife for himself in holiness and honor,* (RSV) *not in passionate lust like the heathen, who do not know God."* It tells us we should know how, or in other words, learn how to take a wife to avoid sexual immorality. Using the correct method of choosing a mate allows someone to avoid sexual immorality. If someone doesn't know the biblical method of choosing a mate, chances are they will do something sexually immoral.

The second point is to have the right relationship with everyone of the opposite sex. Verse 6 *"That no man go beyond* [refers to overstepping a boundary] *and defraud his brother* [Brother not referring to just being male, referring both to men and women, mankind] *in any matter."* Another phase in avoiding sexual immorality comes when one learns how to treat the rest of the opposite-sex, those they will never marry. God has placed a boundary between the brother/sister relationships and the relationship that leads to marriage. Crossing that boundary puts one into sexual immorality. By understanding what that boundary is, a person can avoid that downfall.

To avoid sexual immorality a person must not welcome immoral thoughts. This includes watching movies with sexual scenes and immoral story lines. Music also contains messages that are contrary to God's principle of sexual behavior. To consider these things as acceptable entertainment is harmful. It is amazing how many

Christians subject themselves to sexual immorality in the name of entertainment. To think that such entertainment is not harmful is to deny the fact that God designed us to respond to sexual input.

There are only two ways to live, being guided by the Holy Spirit or by allowing our sinful nature to control us. Romans, chapter 8:1-4, also tells us that through Jesus Christ we have been set free from the law of sin and death. Following God's laws was made impossible because of mankind's inherited sinful nature. But the sacrifice of Jesus for our sins on the cross allowed us to be legally set free from that sinful nature's control.

When people are controlled by their sinful nature their minds are focused on what that nature wants. That is sad, because what our sinful nature wants is always harmful to us and/or to others. It is hostile towards God and His ways.

People who have the Spirit of Christ living in them and are being led by the Holy Spirit are not controlled by their sinful nature. Their minds are focused on what God wants. That focus brings life, peace, and freedom from sin (see Romans 8:9-13). Even though we don't have to be controlled by our sinful nature, it doesn't mean we won't be tempted. James wrote: *"Each one is tempted when, by his own evil desire,* [The temptations will come but that doesn't mean that a person has to give in to them.] *he is dragged away and enticed.* [This is the entertainment of those evil desires, allowing them to linger and not be immediately rejected. Any hesitation in rejecting a tempting thought allows our minds to become fertile ground.] We become predisposed to certain sins because our own evil desires keep us from permanently shutting the door and turning our backs to that sin.

Once this happens sin begins. *Then, after desire has conceived,* [This person has now taken ownership of this desire and it is no longer under consideration; it is now accepted as truth instead of a lie] *it gives birth to sin;* [At this point the corresponding action to these sinful thoughts may or may not take place. It is not necessary to act on thought to be considered in sin. It is impossible, though, to start with a sinful action; such action is always preceded by a sinful thought.] *and sin, when it is full-grown, gives birth to death"* (James 1:14-15). The death referred to here is not always exclusively the end of physical life. It more often refers to something being destroyed. Sin will always cause a loss of something. The Bible tells us that *"the wages* [what we have earned] *of sin is death"* (see Romans 6:23).

Deceived into Lust

One reason some are deceived into not avoiding such sexual immorality is that they mistake the term lust as meaning the "desire" to have sex. That desire is normal and they wouldn't want to give up sex altogether, so they convince themselves that sex is not something to stay away from. But lust is not just the desire for sex, it is the greed for wrong sex. Lust is craving affections that God doesn't want you to fulfill. Lust is wanting something you shouldn't have. Having sex does not make lust go away Marriage cannot fulfill lust, **nothing** can. Someone who gets married with a lust problem doesn't lose it because he/she gets married. It is better to never experience lust at all. Cut it off right in its beginning stages. *"Flee also youthful lusts:* [Youthful lust is not something that is exclusive to a younger age group, it is talking about lust at its beginning stages] *but follow righteousness, faith, charity, peace, with them that call on the Lord out of a pure heart"* (2 Tim 2:22 KJV).

Sexual immorality is a very serious problem. It is a major factor in the divorce epidemic. It has ruined lives and homes. We will never be able to stop all sexual immorality, but we can prevent it from happening in the lives of those who want to avoid it. We can do that by educating people in what biblical sexual morality is, thus arming them against any unintentional violations. As Christians we have the responsibility to instruct our brothers and sisters in this area. There is absolutely no substitute for that.

CHAPTER 10

UNEQUALLY YOKED

Following the Command

Second Corinthians 6:14 tells Christians they should not be unequally yoked with unbelievers. The validity of that command should not be subject to discussion, debate, or situational ethics. Years ago I was trying to explain to a woman the hazards of becoming unequally yoked in marriage. She quickly dismissed the idea because she knew someone who had gotten married to an unbeliever and it had worked out all right for that couple. While this may be a testimony to God's grace in that situation, it is only an excuse for disobedience for the person I was talking to.

To follow the command, we must know what it means to be unequally yoked. It does not mean you shouldn't have any contact or association with unbelievers. *"I have written you in my letter not to associate with sexually immoral people not at all meaning the people of this world who are immoral, or the greedy and swindlers, or idolaters. In that case you would have to leave this world"* (1 Corinthians 5:9-10). According to the Williams translation, being unequally yoked means you are forming intimate and inconsistent relationships with unbelievers (see 2 Cor 6). The problem comes in the **type** of relationship we are having with unbelievers. Certain relationships, such as marriage, require unity. Having a marriage relationship that is not unified is an inconsistent relationship.

"Be not unequally yoked in marriage" is a preventive command that should be applied only to single adults. This command serves no purpose to those already married. God doesn't want a marriage to break up because one spouse is an unbeliever. He is not the author of such confusion (see 1 Cor 14:33 KJV). *"To the rest I say this (I, not the Lord): If any brother has a wife who is not a believer and she is willing to live with him, he must not divorce her. And if a woman has a husband who is not a believer and he is willing to live with her, she must not divorce him"* (1 Corinthians 7:12-13).

As with all of God's commands there is a whole lot more to violating His instruction than just breaking a rule. The reason for or the motive behind breaking the rule is just as important to God as breaking the rule. *To not be unequally yoked with an unbeliever is not just an arbitrary command; there are reasons and concerns for it.*

Sin is more than doing the wrong thing. It's breaking fellowship with the Lord. Hating sin is meaningless without understanding how it affects our personal relationship with our heavenly Father.[5] At what point are you willing to break fellowship with God? Repent over what sin has done to your relationship with Him, not just over the sin itself. *"Yet now I am happy, not because you were made sorry, but because your sorrow led you to repentance. For you became sorrowful as God intended and so were not harmed in any way by us. Godly sorrow brings repentance that leads to salvation and leaves no regret, but worldly sorrow brings death"* (2 Corinthians 7:9-10).

Wanting to be unequally yoked is a red flag denoting a serious problem. It is not simple disobedience. For those who willingly decide to disobey, this is evidence of a problem in their relationship

---

[5] Growing Families International.

with God. Why would a Christian want to be unequally yoked when God explicitly tells them not to be? There must be some darkness in them that attracts them to darkness.

Reasons and Concerns for the Command

The reason God gave the command is threefold: it protects people from heartache and other difficulties in life; it helps to fulfill one of the purposes for marriage which is to produce godly children (see Mal 2:15); and it prevents a decline of a person's relationship with God. People who are already unequally yoked in marriage face many struggles. One of the most prevalent is what Church do they both attend and which belief gets taught to their children? I have seen so many women who attend services with their children, grieved by the fact that their husband isn't sharing in the most important part of their life—their faith in Jesus Christ. This is the person people who are contemplating marrying an unbeliever should talk to. Let them explain to her why they think it is all right to marry an unbeliever when she would give anything to see her marriage equally yoked.

Some Christians enter into a relationship with a non-Christian with the idea that this will win the non-believer over to Christ. I have heard this approach sometimes referred to as "missionary dating." This approach seldom works as intended and more often than not it has the opposite effect. *"Do not be deceived: Bad company ruins good morals"* (1 Cor 15:33 RSV). I have heard it said, "If you run with dogs you will eventually bark."

The cause behind the struggles in an unequally yoked marriage is found in 2 Corinthians 6:14 in five questions asked.

1. *"For what do righteousness and wickedness have in common?"* and in the Phillips translation: *"What common interest can there be between goodness and evil?"* The answer, of course, is **Nothing**.

One of the reasons believers choose to disobey this command is not because they are trying to do something wrong. They just don't see a big difference between themselves and unbelievers. Either God has never been allowed to make a big difference in their lives or He at one time made a big difference but double-mindedness has crept in. *"An oracle is within my heart concerning the sinfulness of the wicked: There is no fear of God before his eyes. For in his own eyes he flatters himself too much to detect or hate his sin"* (Psalm 36:1-2).

Being double-minded is an attempt to combine light and darkness. An example is the two bumper stickers on the same car I saw recently. One said, " Real Men Love Jesus;" the other advertised the call letters of a worldly radio station. James tells us that double-minded people shouldn't even think they will receive anything from the Lord. *"If any of you lacks wisdom, he should ask God, who gives generously to all without finding fault, and it will be given to him. But when he asks, he must believe and not doubt, because he who doubts is like a wave of the sea, blown and tossed by the wind. That man should not think he will receive anything from the Lord; he is a doubleminded man, unstable in all he does"* (James 1:5-8).

2. *"What fellowship can light have with darkness?"* The answer is it is impossible to have true fellowship in that situation. Darkness and light cannot fellowship. Darkness can only fellowship with darkness; light can only fellowship with light. *"But if we walk in the light, as he is in the light, we have fellowship with one another, and the blood of Jesus, his Son, purifies us from all sin"* (1 Jn 1:7). The Phillips translation puts it this way: *"How can light and darkness share life together?"*

How can a believer say he or she values something as important as salvation, or believe it to be absolutely necessary if he/she wants to unite with someone who doesn't believe in having a relationship with Jesus Christ? This personal belief demonstrates what is important to them and where their priorities are.

3. *"What harmony is there between Christ and Belial?"* Belial refers to Satan's banner that is inscribed with the word "worthlessness." It is an abomination to suggest that Christ would wave Satan's banner. There will never be harmony between Jesus Christ and that banner waving. He violently opposes Satan.

4. *"What does a believer have in common with an unbeliever?"* Very little! Their outlook on life—what they think and talk about, and what they spend their time and money on—should be completely different. The believer will be interested in advancing the kingdom of God, the unbeliever won't be. The believer will be obsessed with pleasing God, the unbeliever won't even care about such things. I realize this isn't always the case, but it should be. It is impossible to have dual loyalty in our relationship with the Almighty. And there isn't a third choice. *"No one can serve two masters. Either he will hate the one and love the other, or he will be devoted to the one and despise the other. You cannot serve both God and Money"* (Matt 6:24).

5. *"What agreement is there between the temple of God and idols?"* There isn't any agreement between these two. *"For we are the temple of the living God. As God has said: 'I will live with them and walk among them, and I will be their God, and they will be my people.'"* Amos 3:3 puts it this way: *"How can two walk together unless they be agreed?"* The obvious answer to that question is, they can't.

What is wrong about a marriage between a believer and an unbeliever? The couple would find they have little in common, little to fellowship about, little harmony, and little to agree on. This is an incomplete marriage at best. The highest relationship that can occur at that point is one of camaraderie. Although possible, it is difficult to sustain a marriage at that level of relationship.

One of the keys to not getting divorced is never marry someone who believes in divorce. An unbeliever cannot honor God's institution of marriage the way that a believer can. There will always be something missing in the respect that God requires. Marriage is a biblical union, not a social event.

So, what should we do? Verse seventeen of Second Corinthians tells us, "*Therefore* [this is the conclusion from the previous information] *come out from them and be separate, says the Lord.*" The word translated "separate" in the Greek means to set off by boundary, limit, exclude, appoint, divide, sever. The Moffatt translation translates verse seventeen as, "*'Therefore come away from these separate. Touch no unclean thing, and I will receive you. I will be a Father to you, and you will be my sons and daughters, says the Lord Almighty' (v.18). Since we have these promises, dear friends, let us purify ourselves from everything that contaminates body and spirit, perfecting holiness out of reverence for God*" (2 Corinthians 7:1).

Once again prevention is the key. Apply this commandment to prevent an unequally yoked marriage, but do not condemn those who are already unequally yoked. Understand the value of preventing the problems caused by violating this command. Prevent these problems from happening by training your child to never even think of desiring a romantic relationship with an unbeliever. If your child never enters into a romantic relationship with an unbeliever he or she will never marry one. Those who do, run the risk of being married to one. Keep in mind that if there is a temptation to do so this indicates a problem in a person's relationship with God. They should run for help!

"Do not be yoked together with unbelievers. For what do righteousness and wickedness have in common? Or what fellowship can light

have with darkness? What harmony is there between Christ and Belial? What does a believer have in common with an unbeliever? What agreement is there between the temple of God and idols? For we are the temple of the living God. As God has said: "I will live with them and walk among them, and I will be their God, and they will be my people. Therefore come out from them and be separate, says the Lord. Touch no unclean thing, and I will receive you. I will be a Father to you, and you will be my sons and daughters, says the Lord Almighty."

—2 Cor 6:14-18

"Stop forming intimate and inconsistent relations with unbelievers."

—2 Cor 6:14 Williams translation

CHAPTER 11

PURITY'S
FUTURE BENEFITS

Related Events of Life

All of a child's training should point to one thing, preparing a child to become a mature adult. It is at this time the benefits of moral purity will pay even greater dividends. Every principle I have shared to this point should be applied not only for the purpose of blessing a child while they are becoming an adult, but ultimately once they are an adult. Preparing your child to become a morally pure adult requires looking ahead and understanding what it is you are trying to accomplish.

Life is a progression of building blocks not a series of unrelated events. A philosophy of some parents is that the only purpose a child has in life is just to have fun. We shouldn't give them any chores or train them in anything, just let them have fun. Then those same children become teens and the same mentality says, "Oh, those are special years, just let them have fun." Then they become single adults eighteen years and older and then the thinking becomes, "You've got to let them have many relationships because one of these days they are going to be tied down to just one." Then these spoiled and irresponsible people get married and the wife says to the husband, "We need to get such and such done." The husband says, "Well, after my Nintendo, and the game on TV…Oh, not today, I don't have time." It's no wonder, the guy can't find time to do his chores, he's been trained to seek after pleasure all his life. All of a sudden, he gets married and faces a reality check. Marriage is not strictly for pleasure. Unfortunately, the man has been brought up in a society with a totally unrealistic and destructive philosophy. The theme for today seems to be to remain a child for as long as possible. There is no preparation for the road ahead and a complete disregard for the need to transition through the different stages of life. You wonder why there are so many problems in marriage? It's because people don't look at the big picture.

People talk about their dating life, their sex life, their thought life, their private life, as if all were isolated and separate. They view singleness as an isolated state, unrelated to any other part of life. This is a schizophrenic concept if I ever heard one. We are only one person so whatever we do in any area of our life impacts us in other areas.

Being single is a part of life just like other aspects of life are. God's intertwined His plan for singleness with all areas of our life. You can't separate singleness from the whole life package. What a person does in their singleness doesn't affect just their time of being single. It also determines what kind of person they will become and what kind of marriage they will have. Biblical singleness not only changed my life as a single person, it also affected me after I got married, and later when I became a parent.

If used correctly biblical singleness has tremendous implications. Not only will it change the single person's life it will also change the lives of those around them. *By God's design, biblical singleness provides a powerful benefit to everyone.* The following are five ways in which biblical singleness benefits the single person and others:

1. The maturing of the person.
2. The effective operation of the Church.
3. The strengthening of already existing families.
4. Marital success.
5. Better parent.

Number Two Priority

The picture of what biblical singleness looks like is found in the comparison God makes between those who are married and those who are single. He says, *"I would like you to be free from concern. An unmarried man is concerned about the Lord's affairs–how he can please the Lord. But a married man is concerned about the affairs of this world–how he can please his wife–and his **interests** are divided"* (1 Cor 7:32-34). One biblical difference between a single person and a married person should be found in their number two priority. God makes this distinction by telling us that those who are single should not have their interests divided. *Interests* in this verse refers to the things a person values most, what a person has as his/her greatest concern. It refers to what he or she has an affection for, is involved in, and where the most time, energy, and resources are spent —second only to the relationship to God. Our personal relationship with the Father should be our number one priority. But for singles, the second priority can and should be devoted to acts of service to the Lord. Those who are married should have their interests divided between service and family (v. 34). This is not a bad thing. It is appropriate to give time and energy to family needs.

Let's visualize the number two priority concept in the shape of a pie. I'll call it the Priority Passion Pie. For those who are married or are single parents, the pie is divided into two pieces—one part family responsibility, the other outreach ministry. The ratio changes between the two depending on family dynamics. If there are young children, family responsibility becomes the majority of the pie. If the children are grown, then the ministry section expands. In contrast for those not married the pie is undivided; it is all outreach ministry. Singleness should be a time dedicated to serving others on the Lord's behalf. I am not saying, however, that everyone-whether married or single –should neglect family responsibilities toward parents or siblings. Many people today think the single pie is free of responsibility, empty of meaning, and full of free time. But that is not what the Bible says should be the case. First Corinthians 7:35 refers to undistracted, undivided devotion to the Lord. The single pie has no divisions in it.

Although each person has twenty-four hours to use each day, individual responsibilities differ. Singles do not have more time; they have more **discretionary** time and that time must be filled with ministry responsibilities. God does not consider it free time.

It's biblical and extremely important that we keep our priorities in order. Bad things happen when people allow their number two priority to get out of order. We all have heard of the much-publicized problems of ministers who get so involved in ministries that their families are neglected and things fall apart. The Bible asks, *"If anyone does not know how to manage his own family, how can he take care of God's Church?"* (1 Tim 3:5). But the same problem in priority mismanagement can happen to anyone.

Singles have to fight to keep from having their pie divided. There is competition for your number two priority just like there is for your number one. A multitude of distractions are waiting to come in and divide the pie. The greatest distraction comes from unbiblical male/female relationships. Opposite-sex relationships have become the number one preoccupation of most teen and young adult singles today. This preoccupation is harmful because it diverts the love, passion and attention that should be directed toward God and not to other people. This will dull the appetite for serving God. The world's system promotes this preoccupation, but as you can see it is destructive.

In my years of ministry I have seen the same scenario over and over again. An on-fire Christian who is excited about God and doing great things but is lacking in understanding about godly relationships, gets involved with the wrong person and is dragged away, leaves the Church, and loses that dynamic relationship with God. The #1 weapon the devil uses against those who are single is tempting them to enter into unbiblical relationships with the opposite sex. This battle is not something that can be taken lightly.

To avoid that trap, single people must understand and believe four things;

1. God has a specific plan for their life.
2. They must know they can trust God with their desire to get married. If marriage is part of His plan for them, then that plan includes a specific person he/she is to marry. God also calls a few to remain single and that is an awesome calling, one to be highly respected.
3. It is unnecessary to search for a mate. God is the one who arranges the meeting that brings two people together.
4. Anyone who is not the specific person God intends for the single to marry must be treated in the same manner as a natural sibling.

This plan of belief allows tremendous freedom to the single; he/she can minister instead of wasting lots of unproductive time. Obviously, all of these beliefs run contrary to our society's focus, but, then, so do most of Christianity's tenets!

Many Christians have been misled into believing that being single and being lonely are synonymous. Often at weddings we hear the quotation, "It is not good for man to be alone." I just want you to know that that line from Genesis, chapter two, has been taken out of context. It is sometimes used as justification to be involved in relationships God never intended. The verse says, *"The Lord God said it is not good for the man to be alone..."* (Gen 2:18). God identified the need for Adam to have a mate, it wasn't Adam complaining he was lonely. It wasn't Aunt Tilly who said that he shouldn't be alone, or the pastor, or any of his friends. God said it, and that fact is important.

Next we have to understand to **whom** God was referring. He was referring to **the man**, not "man" as used in the general sense. We can't insert any name here, as people often do. I have consulted and compared the top seven translations of the Bible, and five out of seven translate this verse as: *"It is not good for THE man to be alone."* If you look up "the man" in the Hebrew, it literally refers to Adam. The reason God knew it wasn't good for Adam to be alone was because God knew that Adam would sin and He had to provide a way of escape for him. The Bible refers to Jesus as the Lamb that was slain from the creation of the world (see Rev 13:8). God knew in advance that Adam would sin and mankind would need a savior. If He hadn't brought Eve into existence, there would have been no way for a Savior to be born; therefore, this wouldn't have been good.

Some say it is not good that man not get married because of his loneliness. If that's the case, then Jesus did something that wasn't good when He didn't marry, and we know that's not true. We also know, from other Scriptures, that in some cases not being married was a good thing. *"Now for the matters you wrote about: It is good for a man not to marry"* (1 Cor 7:1).

All good Bible students know that you need two or three witnesses for a biblical truth to be established. *"Every matter must be established by the testimony of two or three witnesses"* (2 Cor 13:1). In light of that fact, are there any other Scriptures saying it is not good for man to be alone, interpreting "alone" as meaning not married? No! So we shouldn't take that verse in 1 Corinthians and use it out of context.

Scripture also says, *"Brothers, each man, as responsible to God, should remain in the situation God called him to"* (1 Cor 7:24). Therefore, it is important for single adults to find contentment in their present circumstances. They need to have faith in the fact that God has a purpose for their singleness. By focusing on becoming a blessing to others, when God does bring the specific mate into their life the person can make a healthy contribution to the relationship, instead of being a drain on it.

Some who are single try to solve their loneliness by becoming involved in a relationship or, even worse, a series of them. Not only is this relationship a problem in itself, it is also a symptom of a deeper problem: they are not allowing God to be the fulfillment of their lives. They are looking for love in the wrong places, rather than looking to Him to meet their need. All of us—married or single—should be placing our focus on our relationship with God.

Understanding this concept allows singles a choice of what to do when they are alone, and it allows them to use their alone time for good. Have you ever heard anyone say, "I'm bored"? Well, if you look up the word "bored" in Hebrew and in Greek it translates to the same thing: *I'm not doing what God wants me to do!*

Benefits of Biblical Singleness

Singleness should be an exclusive time during which one develops a deeper personal relationship with God. There will never be a better opportunity to build a firm foundation for this relationship. It is easier for a person to handle one major relationship than handling two of them. I am not saying that singleness is the only time for growth, but if this opportunity is available, take advantage of it!

There's a lie circulating out there that says, " I can't wait to get married because my mate will be able to help me get my relationship with God together." Or, "When I'm married, I'll be able to do that ministry God has called me to." The truth is that it's easier to develop a personal relationship with God and grow in ministry when a person is single. Marriage has a part to play concerning growth in these two areas, but a person shouldn't try to pawn off the growing responsibility on someone else.

What should we do to build a strong relationship with God? We should have private time between us and God, a time dedicated to prayer and Bible study. Studying the Bible is not just the pastor's duty, it is essential for every Christian to know the Bible well. We all need true friendship and intimacy with the Father. Nothing should be more important; nothing should be a higher priority!

Focus Shift

Building a strong relationship with God focuses the single's attention on others. The natural outcome of a personal relationship with God is the overwhelming responsibility one feels to serve others. As a person's relationship with God improves, so also does their relationship with others; these go hand-in-hand. It's impossible to know God in a true way and not want to serve other people. *"If anyone says, 'I love God,' yet hates his brother, he is a liar. For anyone who does not love his brother, whom he has seen, cannot love God, whom he has not seen"* (1 John 4:20).

You will never have a better relationship with any person than the level of relationship you have with the Lord. Let's say your relationship with God is a nine, then you cannot have a better relationship with any other person that's higher than an eight. If your relationship with God is a two, you can't have a better relationship with people than a one! The basis is: If you can't have a great relationship with the perfect God, how can you expect to have a great relationship with someone who is not perfect?

Effective Operation of the Church

Another important reason for biblical singleness is the effective operation of the Church. Those who are single should make up a greater portion of the work force in Church ministry. If single people followed 1 Corinthians 7:32-35 over half of the ministry work in the Church would be done by them. This time of service should be voluntary, not forced by leadership. The service does not come as a command from the Church but as the fruit of the Church's obligation to teach the truth about singleness. The fuel for such a productive single life is the freeing power of the gospel (see John 8:32).

If the truth is taught, the fruit will follow—single adults will be energized and have a desire to serve. As their relationship with God grows, good things will follow. Just think about all the wasted time used on unbiblical opposite-sex relationships and how that time could be better used for God's kingdom. Pastors, unless you are already turning away people offering to help in your Church, you are missing that opportunity by not implementing this truth!

Single adults who divide their pie correctly take the pressure off those who are married. This allows parents to fulfill their commitment to what God has called them to, particularly the discipling of their children. Not dividing the priority passion pie correctly weakens the family unit. Singles who divide the pie incorrectly, force another person to fulfill their responsibility. They often cause those who are married to not divide the pie at all or to divide it into wrong portions and not give enough time to family. Both the singles dividing the pie and the married people dividing the pie incorrectly weaken the family unit.

Marriage Preparation

Another one of the purposes of biblical singleness is preparation for marriage. It serves as the foundation in the building process for marriage. People who think they can have a great marriage without having a great singleness are like those thinking they don't need to pay attention to what is being taught in the sixth grade because they will pick it up in the ninth grade. Adam was not created married; he was single. So, God has a purpose in singleness. It teaches *servanthood and selflessness*, both of which are necessary for marriage. Marriage preparation includes everything a person does before the ceremony. On the day I got married I did not stand before my wife promising to someday be a great Christian. I was bringing to her everything I had done up to that point. All God had already done in my life could be a gift to her! I had become a certain person because of what God had done. I was not a "project" for her to shape into a perfect mate.

What prepared me for marriage and fatherhood was all of those hours and hours I had spent witnessing and serving people. Imagine all those difficult questions I was being asked by complete strangers! They made me study in a deeper way so I was able to answer them the next time. Not one ounce of time and effort put into that preparation has gone to waste. I now have my three precious daughters who are asking simplistic yet difficult questions and, because of my past experiences, I am able to answer them. Learning how to witness and to serve people during my singleness built a foundation for my life now.

Some wrongly believe that marriage preparation should begin once they meet that special someone. Others falsely believe that as long as they have no immediate interest in marriage, it's so far in the future, that any preparation can be put off until a later date. And others even think that if they don't know if they will ever get married, they don't have to concern themselves with it at all. This attitude is a major cause of many marital problems. Waiting until the last minute to prepare for something important never works. It is like a commercial pilot waiting until take-off to read the instruction manual. It takes years of preparation through godly singleness to prepare for a successful marriage.

The good news is that we can teach and disciple in the biblical purpose of singleness. We must help our singles to fight against the currently accepted practice of having unbiblical relationships with the opposite sex. It is the primary weapon the devil uses against those who are single. That battle lies with all of us because everyone can benefit from obedient singles. As the singles mature, they foster marital success, strengthen already existing families and enhance the effective operation of the Church. Singleness can be a powerful tool in the hands of God. There are no boundaries or limitations for a single person in what he or she has the opportunity to do for Him. What an exciting adventure in God for those who consciously decide to move into the role waiting for them. There is no doubt that God has designed singleness and has gifted it with power! Parents who have raised their children with the goal of purity and becoming a mature adult, can expect the *rewards* that biblical singleness brings.

MY MATE IS

I WROTE THIS POEM ABOUT
MY WIFE BEFORE I EVER MET HER.

When I considered what my mate should be,
I made a list and said, "This is for me.

Oh God, get me one please,
What I need in my life is one of these."

I had to make sure He wouldn't mess up my life,
By sending me a no-good kind of wife.

Oh, the kind of trust I have shown.
The plan for my life I had not known.

God said, "He would give me the desires of my heart."[6]
To use my plan, rather than His, wouldn't be very smart.

---

[6] Psalm 37:4

Seeing the difference between God's and mine,
I can create false desires by giving someone attention and time.

The time before He said, "Let there be light,"[7]
He knew all of my needs and met them all right.

My story is no different than Adam's you see.
Just as Adam had to give of himself willingly.

I, too, must surrender some flesh surrounding my heart,
Give it to God and exchange it for the right part.

With all of the animals Adam could see,
There was not one helpmeet fit for him.

A part of him they could never fill,
The part that was taken only will.

As soon as he saw her it was divinely known,
"This is flesh of my flesh and bone of my bones."[8]

Before he knew Eve he could have made up his mind,
So far this animal is the best I can find.

Don't limit your mate to just those you know.
There's someone out there, trust God to show.

She was there all of the time.
I didn't just find her, she was already mine.

I was so surprised, "Look what I found!"
God wasn't blind—He knew she was around.

---

[7] Genesis 1:3
[8] Genesis 2:23

He's always working in people's lives,
To get them together to be husbands and wives.

A tremendous burden has been lifted from me,
"Seek not a wife,"[9] is the Bible's plea.

"Unless God builds a house a man labors in vain."[10]
Why waste your time with something God didn't ordain?

The compromise in our daily lives we make,
Will determine our ability to find the true,
or be cursed with the fake.

Yes, we have a part that is ours to play,
We can determine if God gets His way.

He gave us a free will; it's ours to choose,
With all God has for us, we still can refuse.

I pray that you would be active in sharing your faith.
Understanding comes from doing, and knowing it was His grace.

Don't wait until your wedding day to get it together,
You'll fulfill the vow of worser and not for the better.

The best of friends can be separated by a thing called pride.
"Lust won't hinder my love for her." Buddy you just lied.

Don't practice lust and unfaithfulness,
I don't care how long you've been waiting,
Good harvest you'll reap if you sow good seed without fainting.

---

[9] 1 Corinthians 7:27
[10] Psalm 127:1

Be the one before you find the one:
Be a blessing rather than a curse; you'll find it's a lot more fun.
Determine right now, "I want to be a blessing."
There is a lot more to that than claiming and confessing.

We need to let God's spirit guide,
Being faithful in the little things, so the bigger God can provide.

There is no beauty that can buy my half,
It's not just that she can cook or make me laugh.

The only requirement for my mate is:
She was from the beginning of time and just plain is.

And if there's someone out there you have found.
You know what I'm telling you, but you're still feeling down.

Don't try to tell me that you're lovesick;
You're using two words that contradict.

A hurting sometimes you feel inside,
You need God's Word to make a divide.

Any torment that you could go through,
Isn't from God let me tell you.

Feelings may push and emotions may shove,
But get your guidance from God above.

Love has in it no element of fear,[11]
Because fear has torment, that's so clear.

A perfect love will cast fear aside,[12]
Let peace rule your heart and be your guide.

---

[11] 1 John 4:18
[12] 1 John 4:18

Now if you read this and you're still all depressed,
Because of what you've done before, you made a mess.

Comfort is still found in this message today:
God's got a plan, and Jesus is the Way.

The rules of mathematics can all be ignored,
The wisdom of God is to be explored.

What do you think of three that equals one?
Sacrificing a Son so that many will come?

God is big enough to handle our mistakes,
Giving your care to Jesus is what it takes.

Starting all over is something God knows how to do,
Your tragedy has ended if you believe for the brand new.

"Therefore shall a man leave his father
and mother, and cleave to his wife,"[13]
They shall fulfill a special course, God's plan for their life.

Selecting your father and mother you had no choice,
But when leaving that family and choosing
your own, please hear God's voice.

Leaving your family of natural birth,
Cleaving to a family born in God's Spirit
and manifesting it in the earth.

"Thank you Tom for writing this poem,
It's very entertaining, but it doesn't hit home.
I've believed this for several years,
It sounds so good, but I am still left with tears.

---

[13] Genesis 2:24

But I'm happy for you that you believe this way,
As for me this may never happen, especially today."

You mean to tell me that you're a special case,
One of those not under His grace.?

When God's promises don't come true,
There's someone at fault, and I'll pick you.

You don't need to question Him, I'll tell you why,
It's just impossible for God to lie.

Too many times we've said we have done all we can do,
But really have stopped at the point we wanted to.

How much effort will you put in,
To change your life and get rid of sin?

This is no time to hang your head,
Forget self-pity and do what He said.

He never promised us things we can't do,
Buddy-up with God, you'll make it through.

He said with this world He has made amends.
Nothing wrong with that relationship, it's us to
Him that we need to make friends.

God's got a plan in the things He did start,
He didn't do it haphazardly; He did it from His heart.

**For books or questions
please contact Tom at
singlepurposeministries.org**

LaVergne, TN USA
10 August 2010
192668LV00003B/34/A